CHINESE
SELF-TAUGHT

CHINESE
SELF-TAUGHT

BY THE NATURAL METHOD

WITH

PHONETIC PRONUNCIATION
(THIMM'S SYSTEM)

JOHN DARROCH

SECOND EDITION

GYAN

Published by

Gyan Publishing House
5, Ansari Road
Daryaganj, New Delhi-110002
Phone: 011-47034999, 9811692060
E-mail: books@gyanbooks.com

Distribution Network
gyanbooks.com
India, USA, Canada, UK, Australia, France

ISBN : 978-81-212-4262-2 (HB)
First Published, London, 1914

2nd Impression 2020

Printed at: Gyan Press, Delhi.

Chinese Self-Taught
Author: John Darroch

Marlborough's Self-Taught Series.

Chinese Self-Taught

by the Natural Method.

WITH

Phonetic Pronunciation.

TRADE MARK REGISTERED

THIMM'S SYSTEM.

BY

JOHN DARROCH, Litt.D.,

Chairman of the Executive Committee of the Educational Association of China;
General Agent of the Religious Tract Society in China.

SECOND EDITION.

Companion Volume
"CHINESE GRAMMAR SELF-TAUGHT."

PRINTED IN GREAT BRITAIN

LONDON:
E. MARLBOROUGH & Co. LTD., 51 Old Bailey, E.C.4

PUBLISHERS' NOTE.

THIS manual of Chinese is designed to serve the double purpose of a text-book for students, officers, civil servants, missionaries, &c., and a handbook for tourists, travellers, and other temporary visitors to the vast country of China, with the exception perhaps of the southern ports referred to in the opening pages.

The Rev. J. Darroch, Litt.D., the Author, is the Chairman of the Executive Committee of the *Educational Association of China*; he has spent many years amongst the Mandarin-speaking population, and the results of his long experience are embodied in these volumes, being thus placed at the service of all who require to become acquainted with the Chinese language.

For those whom the pleasure of travel or the calls of trade and commerce bring into touch with the native Chinese, a very comprehensive vocabulary of necessary and useful words is supplied, together with corresponding collections of colloquial phrases and sentences equally practical and useful in character. These are all classified under subject-titles for easy reference, and the phonetic pronunciation of the Chinese words, written in accordance with Marlborough's popular system of phonetics, is placed under the Romanised form of the words given in the third column. Thus, a tourist, traveller, or trader can readily make himself understood amongst the Chinese by means of this Manual.

The opening section supplies an explanation of the pronunciation of Chinese, the tones, and the scheme of phonetics adopted, and will be found to obviate the difficulties that arise in acquiring the language. These pages should therefore be read with every care and attention. At the same time no opportunity should be lost of hearing the language spoken by an educated native of China.

Chinese Grammar Self-Taught,* by the same Author, is a companion volume to the present work, and the two books together will be found a most useful and practical introduction to the Chinese language, spoken, written, and printed.

London, 1914.

* **Chinese Grammar Self-Taught,** by J. Darroch, Litt.D., O.B.E., uniform with *Chinese Self-Taught.* For home study and class use. Red Cloth 7/6. Blue Wrapper 6/-. *Chinese Self-Taught and Grammar* in one volume, Cloth 12/6. London: E. Marlborough & Co., Ltd.

CONTENTS.

CHINESE SELF-TAUGHT

SYLLABARY AND PRONUNCIATION

Language of China

China is an Empire of such vast extent that it may justly be called a continent rather than a kingdom. Naturally, there are many dialects spoken in different parts of the country and yet there is undeniably a Chinese language current throughout the whole of China. This is usually called the Mandarin or official language and is the spoken language—with local variations—of the great mass of the Chinese people. Of the 400,000,000 Chinese probably 350,000,000 speak Mandarin; the remaining 50,000,000 speak more than 20 different dialects all having a more or less distant resemblance to the official language.

Area in which Mandarin is Spoken

Mandarin is spoken from the China Sea to the borders of Burmah and from Manchuria in the north to a considerable distance south of the river Yangtse. But as one travels south from the great river the language grows more and more corrupt until it becomes absolutely unintelligible to a native speaking the pure Mandarin of northern China.

The Provinces in which Mandarin is not spoken stretch southward from Shanghai along the coast to the frontiers of Tongking. They are Chehkiang, Fuhkien and Kwantung. Tourists will therefore understand that no spoken phrase from this book is likely to be understood in Hong-kong, Canton, Amoy, Foochow or any of the southern ports. Each of these places has a totally different dialect from its neighbours and it is not possible here to do more than attempt to represent by western phonetics the sounds of the one language of China.

Pronunciation of Chinese Words

The English language uses symbols (alphabetic) to represent sounds; the Chinese language uses symbols (ideographs) to represent objects and ideas. As the Chinese ideograph represents imperfectly the object indicated so the letters of our alphabet only imperfectly represent the sound which the reader enunciates. Add to this that the same phonetic symbol represents different sounds to different men, especially so to men of different nationalities, and it will be apparent that our alphabetical symbols are very imperfect media by which to represent foreign and unfamiliar sounds to the eye when no corresponding oral information reaches the mind through the ear.

The Chinese themselves have never represented the characters of their language by any system of phonetic spelling. A Chinese school-master when teaching a pupil the sound of a character will point to the character on the book and say distinctly "WANG." The pupil learns the sound from the lips of the teacher but neither master nor scholar has the faintest notion that it would be possible by any system of caligraphy to write the *sound* of the character.

Romanization

There have been, and are, many systems of representing Chinese symbols by Roman letters. This is called "romanization" and while one or other of the systems is used by every foreigner conversant with Chinese and by Chinese taught in mission schools, the Board of Education has not yet introduced any system of phonetic spelling into Chinese Government schools.

Phonetic Spelling

It is not claimed that the spelling given in this book will enable the student to reproduce the sounds of the Chinese characters with nice exactness. Nevertheless, if the instructions are carefully followed, the speaker will find that he will seldom fail to be understood, and if he can secure the services of a Chinese teacher to read over the tàble of sounds with him he will find little difficulty in mastering thè pronunciation of Chinese.

Appended is a comparative sound table showing three systems of spelling Chinese words. These were each prepared with a different aim and for a different clientele and consequently differ in method.

Sir Thomas Wade's system is that used by the Consular and Customs services in China. It represents northern Mandarin sounds with such fidelity that those accustomed to use it find it perfectly satisfactory. Wade's system was prepared for the use of the English student, already familiar with the phonetic values of the letters used, who would, presumably, have a Chinese teacher at his elbow to aid in the elucidation of any difficulty that might arise.

The second, called "The Standard Romanized System was prepared by a committee of the (missionary) Educational Association of China. Its aim is to teach Chinese illiterates to read their own language in Roman letters instead of in the cumbrous native character. It has been found to be so successful that a bright scholar will master the system and read any book printed in Romanized Chinese after a month's study.

The third follows the "Standard" system in its main outlines but is also based on "Marlborough's phonetic spelling." Its aim is to enable the student who has never heard Chinese spoken to pronounce the words from the printed page with approximate correctness. It must not be supposed that this phonetic system is an attempted improvement on either of the other systems. It is not. It is not so much an attempt to spell the words correctly as an effort to so spell them that a man accustomed only to the erratic pronunciation of English spelling will not pronounce them wrongly. Appended is a Comparative Sound Table in which the three systems are exhibited side by side. A slight study of the parallel columns will show that the three systems are so much alike that anyone who masters one of them will have little difficulty in changing to either of the others should he desire to do so. It will be best for the student to use the phonetic system as long as he has no help, but if he can secure the aid of a Chinese teacher or of one familiar with the Chinese language then it will be better to adopt the Standard system for permanent use.

COMPARATIVE SOUND TABLE

This table shows Sir Thomas Wade's System of Romanization; the Standard Romanized System; and the system of spelling used in this book.

Wade	Standard	Marlborough
A	a	a
Ai	ai	**i**
Ao	ao	ow
Cha	dja	ja
Ch'a	cha	cha
Chai	djai	j**i**
Ch'ai	chai	ch**i**
Chan	djan	jan
Ch'an	chan	chan
Chang	djang	jang
Chao	djao	jow
Ch'ao	chao	chow
Che	dje	jeh
Ch'e	che	cheh
Chên	djen	jun
Ch'ên	chen	chun
Chêng	djeng	jun*g*
Ch'êng	cheng	chun*g*
Chi	gi	gee
Chia	gia	geeah
Ch'ia	chia	cheeah
Chieh	giai	gee**i**
Ch'iai	chiai	chee**i**
Chiang	giang	geeang
Ch'iang	chiang	cheeang
Chiao	giao	giow
Ch'iao	chiao	chiow
Chieh	gieh	ge'eh
Ch'ieh	chieh	che'eh

Wade	Standard	Marlborough
Chien	gien	ge'en
Ch'ien	chien	che'en
Chĭh	djĭ	jirr
Chĭh	chĭ	chirr
Chin	gin	gin
Ching	ging	ging
Ch'ing	ching	ching
Chioh	gioh	geeoh
Ch'ioh	chioh	cheeoh
Chiu	giu	jeeoo
Ch'iu	chiu	cheeoo
Chiung	giung	geeung
Ch'iung	chiung	cheeung
Cho	djo	jo
Ch'o	cho	cho
Chua	djwa	
Ch'ua	chwa	chwa
Ch'wai	chwai	chw**i**
Chuan	djwan	jwan
Ch'uan	chwan	chwan
Chui	djui	jway
Ch'ui	chui	chway
Chun	djwen	jwun
Ch'un	chwen	chwun
Chung	djung	jung
Ch'ung	chung	chung
Chü	gü	geu
Ch'ü	chü	cheu
Chüan	güen	jeuehn

Wade	Standard	Marlborough
Ch'üan	chüen	cheuehn
Chüeh	güeh	jeueh
Ch'üeh	chüeh	cheueh
Chün	gün	jeun
Ch'ün	chün	cheun
Eh	eh	eh
Ên	en	un
Êng	eng	un*g*
Erh	er	ur
Fei	fei	fay
Fên	fen	fun
Fêng	feng	fung
Hai	hai	h**i**
Hao	hao	how
Hei	heh	heh
Hên	hen	hun
Hêng	heng	hun*g*
Hou	hou	hou
Hsi	hsi	shee
Hsia	hsia	sheea
Hsiang	hsiang	sheeang
Hsiao	hsiao	sheeow
Hsieh	hsieh	she'eh
Hsien	hsien	she'en
Hsin	hsin	shin
Hsing	hsing	shing
Hsio	hsioh	sheeoh
Hsiu	hsiu	sheeoo
Hsiung	hsiung	sheung
Hsü	hsü	sheu
Hsüan	hsüen	sheuehn
Hsüeh	hsüeh	sheueh
Hsün	hsün	sheun
Hu	hu	hoo
Huai	hwai	hw**i**
Hui	hwei	hway
Hun	hwen	hwun
Huo	hwo	hwoh
I	i	ee
Jan	ran	ran
Jang	rang	rang
Jê	reh	reh
Jên	ren	run
Jêng	reng	run*g*
Jih	rih	rirr
Jo	roh	roh
Jou	rou	rou
Ju	ru	roo
Jwan	rwan	rwan
Jui	rui	rway
Jun	rwen	rwun
Jung	rung	rung
Kai	gai	gh**i**
K'ai	kai	k**i**
Kan	gan	gan
K'an	kan	kan
Kao	gao	gow
K'ao	kao	kow
Kei	geh	geh
K'ei	keh	keh
Ken	gen	gun
K'en	ken	kun
Kêng	geng	gun*g*
K'êng	keng	kun*g*
Kua	gwa	gwa
K'ua	kwa	kwa
Kuai	gwai	gw**i**
K'uai	kwai	kw**i**
Kuei	gwei	gway
Ku'ei	kuei	kway
Kun	gwen	gwun
K'un	kwen	kwun
Kuo	gwoh	gwoh
K'uo	kuoh	kwoh
Lai	lai	l**i**
Lao	lao	low

Wade	Standard	Marlborough
Lei	lei	lay
Lêng	leng	lun*g*
Li	li	lee
Liang	liang	leeang
Liao	liao	leeow
Lieh	lieh	le'eh
Lien	lien	le'en
Liu	liu	leeoo
Luan	lwan	lwan
Lun	lwen	lwun
Lü	lü	leu
Lüan	lüen	leuehn
Ma	ma	ma
Mai	mai	mī
Mao	mao	mow
Mei	mei	may
Mên	men	mun
Mêng	meng	mung
Mi	mi	mee
Miao	miao	meeow
Mieh	mieh	me'eh
Mien	mien	me'en
Nao	nao	now
Nei	nui	nay
Nên	neng	nun*g*
Niao	niao	neeow
Nieh	nieh	ne'eh
Nien	nien	ne'en
Nioh	nioh	neeoh
Niu	niu	neeoo
O	o	o
Pa	ba	ba
P'a	pa	pa
Pai	bai	bī
P'ai	pai	pī
Pao	bao	bow
P'ao	pao	pow
Pei	bei	bay
P'ei	pei	pay
Pên	ben	bun
P'ên	pen	pun
Pêng	beng	bung
P'êng	peng	pung
Piao	biao	beeow
P'iao	piao	peeow
Pieh	bieh	bee'eh
P'ieh	pieh	pee'eh
Pien	bien	bee'en
P'ien	pien	pee'en
Sai	sai	sī
Sao	sao	sow
Sê	seh	seh
Sêng	seng	sun
Sha	sha	sha
Shai	shai	shī
Shao	shao	show
Shê	shae	shay
Shên	shen	shun
Shêng	sheng	shun*g*
Shih	shĭ	shirr
Shui	shui	shway
Shun	shwen	shwun
Shuo	shwo	shwoh
Ssŭ	szĭ	sizz
Sui	sui	sway
Sun	swen	swun
Tai	dai	dī
T'ai	tai	tī
Tao	dao	dow
T'ao	tao	tow
Tê	deh	deh
T'ê	teh	teh
Têng	deng	dun*g*
T'êng	teng	tun*g*
Ti	di	dee
T'i	ti	tee

Wade	Standard	Marlborough	Wade	Standard	Marlborough
Tiao	diao	deeow	Ts'êng	tseng	tsung
T'iao	tiao	teeow	Tsuan	dzwan	dzwan
Tieh	dieh	dee'eh	Ts'uan	tsuan	tswan
T'ieh	tieh	tee'eh	Tsui	dzui	dzway
Tien	dien	dee'en	Ts'ui	tsui	tsway
T'ien	tien	tee'en	Tsun	dzwen	dzwun
Tiu	diu	deeoo	Ts'un	tswen	tswun
To	do	doh	Tsung	dzung	dzung
T'o	to	toh	Ts'ung	tsung	tsung
Tsa	dzah	dzah	Tzŭ	dzĭ	dze
Ts'a	tsah	tsah	Tz'ŭ	tsĭ	tsze
Tsai	dzai	dzī	Wai	wai	wī
Ts'ai	tsai	tsī	Wei	wei	way
Tsan	dzan	dzan	Wen	wen	wun
Ts'an	tsan	tsan	Yai	yai	yī
Tsang	dzang	dzang	Yao	yao	yow
Ts'ang	tsang	tsang	Yê	yeh	yeh
Tsao	dzao	dzow	Yen	yen	yen
Ts'ao	tsao	tsow	Ying	ying	ying
Tsê	dzeh	dzeh	Yo	yoh	yoh
Ts'ê	tseh	tseh	Yu	yu	you
Tsên	dzen	dzun	Yü	yü	yeu
Ts'ên	tsen	tsun	Yüan	yüen	yeuehn
Tsêng	dzeng	dzung	Yün	yün	yeun

PHONETIC VALUES OF VOWELS USED

Simple Vowels

Phonetic sign.

A, a. Pronounced as in *far;* never as in *fare.* ah, a.

E, e. As the first *e* in *there.* Followed by *n* or *ng* it has the sound of *u* in *fun.*

I, i. As in *pin.* When followed by *e* the sound is as in *pier* (pee-er). ee.

I, i. As in *ice, island* or the pronoun, *I.* i.

Ĭ, ĭ. The sound of this vowel is difficult to represent by any phonetic spelling. It never occurs alone and is found in only six words in the language. These are Djĭ, Chĭ, Shĭ, Szĭ, Dzĭ, and Tsĭ. Szĭ, is pronounced as siz in *sizzle.* In all other combinations ĭ has the sibilant sound of z combined with the preceding consonants. Shĭ, sounds as when one says *Sh! 'hush!.* That is, it has the initial *"sh"* sound and the final sibilant. The other combinations are pronounced similarly. Sometimes, especially in North China, the final vowel sound is irr, or urr. **Djirr, Shirr, etc.** irr.

O, o. As in *go.* oh, o.

U, u. As in *rude.* oo.

Ü, ü. As in German **Bülow.** Perhaps eu, pronounced with the lips pursed and as one sound comes nearest to it in English. eu.

Diphthongs

Ai, ai. As *i* in *island* or the pronoun *I.* i.

Ao, ao. As *ow* in *owl.* ow.

Ei, ei. As *ay* in *lay.* ay.

Ia, ia=ya. Hsia=sheeah. eeah.

Iai, iai.=yeei. (yigh. *igh* **as in** *high*) **Hsiai=sheei.** eei.

Phonetic sign.

Ie, ie=yea. Sie=*say.* yea.

Iu, iu=yeeoo. Shiu is **sheeoo. Liu** is **leeoo,** etc. eeoo.

Oü, ou. As *ou* in *soul* or *ow* in *bow.* ou.

Ui, ui. and **Üe üe** have the sound of *way.* **Lui is lway, Shui, shway,** etc. way.

Words Ending in a Consonant

N and **ng**, are the only consonants in which Chinese words end. **En** has the sound of **un** in **fun. Eng,** the same sound with only a suggestion of the **g** perceptible. un. ung.

Ien. When **en** is preceded by **i** it has the sharp sound of *en* in *pen.* As *ien* in the English words *lenient, transient,* **etc.** Thus, **tien** is not **tyne** nor **teen, but tee'en. Each half of the** word is to be given **the** full **value of the letters** by which it is spelled but the word is a **monosyllable nevertheless. For** instance, the English word *shed* **is a monosyllable composed** of the two distinct sounds *sh-ed* **which are agglutinated** in the complete word *shed.* So in Chinese **the sounds tee-en** agglutinate into the word **tien=tee'en** ee'en.

Tieh, likewise **is not tie** nor **tee,** but **tee'eh.** The two sounds **tee** and **eh** (*eh* as though one were saying *Eh, what?*) agglutinate into the monosyllable **tieh, tee'eh.** eh.

gi, In many parts of South China **the** *g* **is** pronounced hard, **gee** having the sound of *gi* in *give* **but** more generally the sound is soft as **in** *gem.* It makes no difference how the letter is pronounced; either sound being equally correct. **gi** or gh**i** is pronounced like *guy* but **gee**i has the initial sound of gee given above, and the final sound of **i** as in *island.* **Gin, ging,** etc., are either as *gim* in *gimlet* or as in *gimcrack.* in.

Ung, is as in **sung,** but **some** dictionaries represent the sound by **ong.** It is between **o and u.** ung.

Wen is "wun" and combinations like **chwen** retain this sound, the e being as **u** in **fun.** wun.

z, The words spelled by Wade, Chih, Ch'ih, Shih, Ssŭ tzŭ, and tz'ŭ, and in the Standard system djĭ, chĭ, shĭ, sze, dze, and tze, have been referred to above under the vowel **I.** dz.

Phonetic sign.

Sizz, in the phonetic system represents exactly the sound of the word **sze.** In the others the termination is the same sibilant sound as in **sizz:** this termination with the initial dz or ts will give the pronunciation as nearly as possible. sz.

Yüen has the phonetic value of **you** as given above and the final sound of *ain* as in *rain* varying to that of *an* in *ran.* yeuehn.

Yün; same as above with the final sound of *in* in *pin.* yeuin.

Table of Similar but Different Sounds

In reading, endeavour to distinguish clearly the difference between the following sounds.

長 jang,	居 geu,	炒 sha,	須 sheu,
將 jeeang,	去 cheu,	蝦 sheea,	盧 loo,
敞 chang,	除 choo,	上 shang,	留 leeoo,
搶 cheeang,	求 cheoo,	向 sheeang,	驢 leu,
兆 jow,	炒 chow,	少 show,	努 noo,
教 geeow,	巧 cheeow,	小 sheeow,	扭 neeoo,
主 joo,	蟲 chung,	書 shoo,	女 neu.
酒 jeeoo,	窮 cheeung,	休 sheeoo,	

The Aspirate

The aspirate is an important part of a Chinese word. The words to be aspirated are those beginning with the letters Ch, K, P, T, and Ts. The unaspirated form of these sounds are the words beginning with the letters Dj, G, B, D, and Dz. No attention need be paid to these latter sounds beyond enunciating them in a clear natural tone. In pronouncing the aspirated words the breath should be expelled forcibly through the lips while forming the sound. One rule is "Always allow the teeth to part slightly when saying an aspirated word." Notice the difference between the words Jump, Chump. Gall, Call. Bill, Pill, etc. Slightly accentuate the difference of the words beginning with the letters Ch, C, and P, and you have the aspirate.

Most Anglo-Chinese dictionaries represent the aspirate by an inverted comma. They have **ta** and **t'a; cha,** and **ch'a; tsen,** and **ts'en,** etc. In the Standard system of romanization, which is followed in these pages, the unaspirated form of **t** is **represented by d; of ch,** by **g** (generally soft as in **gin**) of **ts**, by **dz**, and **of ch, by dj. So** that the spelling adopted is **da** and **ta; dja,** and **cha; dzen, and tsen,** instead of the older and more ambiguous **method.**

Dj, has the sound of **j** in **Jane; djan is jan; djao is like jow** in **jowl.**

H, is both initial and final. **As initial it is as in English but the** aspirate is emphasized**; it is always a** rough **breathing, sometimes a** guttural. **H, final, is the sign of the last of the five tones. It is not** heard in **Peking but is very marked in mid-China and is exaggerated** in Canton. **In Che** *e* has **the sound of** *e* **in** *there.* **In cheh e has** the sound of *e* **in** *met.* **That is, the sound is abruptly broken off.** In **ta** *a* has the sound of *a* in *far;* in **tah** *a* **has the sound of** *a* **in** *tat.* **In some of the vowel sounds only the shortened form is met** with; e.g. **teh, deh, leh, meh. There is no te, de, le, me. But in ta, da, sa, the shorter form tah, dah, sah, is also common. The** sound **if once heard is easily learned and never forgotten but, as has been said, it is ignored in Peking and North China.**

Note that this use of the letter h in Chinese romanization as indicating the short, abrupt ending of a word is entirely arbitrary. It is exactly the opposite sense to that which the letter usually indicates in English. It is to be remembered, then, that *h* **at the end of a word in the italic letters in the third column of "Chinese Self-taught" is a tone mark;** *h* **in the same column, in Roman letters, follows the accepted English usage: that is, it lengthens the preceding vowel as in ah, oh, etc.**

Exercise on the Aspirates

乍 **ja,**	罷 ba,	帶 di,	袞 **gun,**
岔 cha,	怕 **pa,**	太 **ti,**	捆 **kun,**
皆 geei,	敗 **bi,**	旦 dan,	怪 **gwi,**
差 chi,	派 pi,	探 tan,	快 **kwi,**
展 jan,	播 bo,	敢 gan,	德 deh,
產 chan,	破 po,	砍 kan,	特 **teh,**
坐 dzo,	宗 dzung,	子 dz,	只 **jirr,**
挫 **tso,**	叢 tsung,	此 **tsz,**	恥 **chirr,**

The Tones

The Chinese spoken language has five tones. Each word in the language has its appropriate tone. The tones are even more difficult for the majority of foreigners to master than the aspirates. Many never succeed in distinguishing them except that they have learned from the dictionary that such a word has such a tone. These unmusical people are not necessarily incorrect speakers, for the idiom of a sentence is much more important than the tones of the words of which it is composed, and if the idiom is right the chances are that the sentence will be understood, even if the tones are not absolutely correct. Another point is that even a person with an unmusical ear may yet habitually say the tones correctly. If he has learned his sentences from the lips of a native, he may reproduce accurately the cadence of the sentence without making conscious effort to do so.

The tones are incapable of description. They must be heard to be recognised. Speaking very generally the first tone called "shang-ping" is a low even tone such as one habitually uses in ordinary speech. For this reason in the Standard system of romanization words of this tone are un-marked. All un-marked words are to be understood to be of this tone. The second, or, "sheea-ping" tone is such as one would use if saying "Oh!" in a tone of mild surprise. It is the first tone with the addition of a slightly curved and rising inflexion. The third, the "shang-sheng" tone, is a sharp rising tone with something of acute surprise in it as "Oh, Oh!" The fourth or, "cheu-sheng" tone is a straight forward sound as if one were to say "Go, go!" The fifth or "roo-sheng" tone is found only in words ending in a vowel. These words originally ended in k, p, or t, and still do so in Cantonese and in other Southern dialects. In the North this tone is entirely lost but in Central China the words still retain their abrupt ending without sounding the k, p, or t. This abrupt termination is the "roo-sheng" tone and is indicated as stated above by the letter "h."

Method of Indicating the Tones

For the first or shang-ping tone	˳夫	foo (no mark in romanized spelling)
second or sheea-ping	˳符	fōo
third or shang-sheng	˙腐	fóo

fourth or cheu-sheng	副° fòo
fifth or roo-sheng	福。 foo or fuh. **The final h is the tone mark.**

The method of marking the romanized spelling is that of the Standard system.

The appended exercise on the tones is intended to be read and re-read with a Chinese teacher, the teacher reading the sentence first and the student following and imitating him until he is familiar with the different tones and can tell immediately in which tone a word is said when he hears it.

。氈 chan,	。飛 fay,	。歡 hwan,	。身 shun,
。纏 chān,	。肥 fāy,	。還 hwān,	。神 shūn,
°產 chán,	°匪 fáy,	°緩 hwán,	°審 shún,
懺° chàn,	費° fày,	換° hwàn,	甚° shùn,

。欺 chee,	。孚 foo,	。呵 ho,	。伊 ee,	。[illegible] nee,
。奇 chēe,	。扶 fōo,	。河 hō,	。宜 ēe,	。泥 nēe,
°豈 chée,	°甫 fóo,	°火 hó,	°以 eé,	°你 née,
氣° chèe,	傅° fòo,	貨° hò,	意° eè,	膩° nèe,
泣。 cheeh,	福。 fooh,	喝。 hoh,	一。 eeh,	逆。 neeh,

VOCABULARIES

The World and its Elements

第一課　氣候類

English	Chinese	*Romanized* Pronunciation
Air	空氣	*kung chí* kung chee
cloud	雲	*yün* yeuin
cold	冷	*lèng* lung
darkness	黑暗	*hèh àn* heh an
earth	世界	*shï-giài* sh-geei
east	東	*dung* dung
fire	火	*hwò* hwoh
fog	霧	*wù* woo
frost	霜	*shwang* shwang
hail	雹	*bào* bow
heat	熱	*rèh* reh
light	光	*gwang* gwang
lightning	閃電	*shán-dìen* shan-dee'en
moon	月亮	*yüěh-liàng* yeueh-leeang
north	北	*béh* beh

English	Chinese	Romanized Pronunciation
rainbow	虹	*giang, hung* geeang, hung
shade	陰涼	*yin-liang* yin-leeang
sky	天	*tien* tee'en
south	南	*nàn* nan
stars	星宿	*sing-hsiu* sing-sheeoo
storm	暴風	*bào-fung* bow-fung
sun	太陽	*tài-yang* tī-yang
thaw	化	*hwa* hwah
thunder	打雷	*dá-lei* dah-lay
weather	天氣	*tien-chi* tee'en chee
west	西	*hsi* shee
wind	風	*fung* fung

Land and Water

第二課　　水旱類

English	Chinese	Romanized Pronunciation
Bay	灣	*wan* wan
beach	岸	*àn* an
cliff	崖	*yāi* yī
coast, shore	水邊	*shui-bien* shway-bee'en

English	Chinese	*Romanized* Pronunciation
ice	冰	*bing* bing
island	島	*dáo* dow
lake	湖	*hu* hoo
land	地	*dì* dee
mud	泥	*nǐ* nee
rain	雨	*yü* yeu
river	江	*giang* geeang
rock	磐石	*pan-shǐh* pan-shirr
sea	海	*hái* hi
snow	雪	*hsüeh* sheueh
stream	河	*hō* ho
tide	潮	*chāo* chow
water	水	*shúi* shway
waterfall	瀑布	*bào-bu* bow-boo
wave	浪	*làng* lang
world	世界	*shï-giai* shirr geei

Minerals and Metals

第三課 五行類

English	Chinese	Romanized Pronunciation
Brass	黃銅	*hwang-tung* hwang-tung
bronze	白銅	*beh-tung* beh-tung
cement	水門汀	*shuimending* shway-mun-ding
clay	黃泥	*hwang-ni* hwang-née
coal	煤炭	*mei-tàn* may-tan
concrete	水門汀	*shuimending* shway-mun-ding
copper	紅銅	*hung-tung* hung-tung
diamond	金剛石	*gin-gang-shih* gin-gang-shirr
emerald	綠玉	*lùh-yü* loo-yeu
glass	玻璃	*bo-li* bo-lee
gold	金	*gin* gin
granite	花剛石	*hwa-gang-shih* hwah-gang-shirr
iron	鐵	*tìeh* tee'eh
—, cast	生鐵	*seng-tìeh* sung-tee'eh
—, wrought	熟鐵	*shuh-tìeh* shoo-tee'eh
lead	鉛	*chien* chee'en
lime	石灰	*shìh-hwei* shirr hway
marble	大理石	*dà-lì-shih* dah-lee-shirr
mercury	水銀	*shui-yin* shway-yin

English	Chinese	*Romanized* Pronunciation
Pearl	珍珠	*djen-dju* jun-joo
silver	銀	*yin* yin
slate	石板	*shih bán* shirr-ban
steel	鋼	*gang* gang
stone	石頭	*shìh-tou* shirr-tou
tin	錫	*hsih* shee
zinc	白鉛	*beh-chien* beh-chee'en

Animals, Birds, and Fishes

第四課　　動物類

English	Chinese	*Romanized* Pronunciation
Animal	畜牲	*chuh-seng* choo-sung
barking	狗叫	*góu-giao* gou-geeow
bear	狗熊	*góu-hsiung* gou-sheeung
bird	雀鳥	*chioh-niao* cheeoh-neeow
blackbird	八鵰	*ba-ko* bah-ko
bull	公牛	*gung-niu* gung-new
calf	小牛	*siao-niu* sheeow-new
cat	貓	*mao* mow (ow *as in* owl)

English	Chinese	*Romanized* Pronunciation
Cattle	家畜	*gia-chuh* geeah-choo
chicken	鷄	*gi* gee
cock	公鷄	*gung-gi* gung-gee
cod	鰵魚	*min-yü* min-yeu
cow	牛	*nīu* new
crab	螃蟹	*pang-hsiai* pang-shee
dog	狗	*góu* gou
donkey	驢子	*lü-dz* leu-dz
duck	鴨子	*yàh-dz* ya-dz
eagle	老鷹	*láo-ying* low-ying (ow *as* owl)
eel	黃鱔	*hwang-shàn* hwang-shan
fish	魚	*yü* yeu
fox	狐狸	*hu-li* hoo-lee
goat	山羊	*shan-yang* shan-yang
goose	鵝子	*o-dz* oh-dz
grouse	鵄鳩	*djï-giu* jirr-jeeoo
hair, of head	頭髮	*tou-fàh* tou-fa (fa *as in* fat)
hair	毛	*mao* mow (ow *as in* owl)
hen	母鷄	*mú-gi* moo-gee
herd	羣	*chün* cheun
herring	青鱗魚	*ching-lin-yü* ching-lin-yeu

English	Chinese	*Romanized* Pronunciation
Hoof	蹄子	*ti-dz* tee-dz
horse	馬	*má* mah
lamb	羔羊	*gao-yang* gow-yang
lark	叫天鳥	*giào-tien-niao* geeow-tee'en-neeow
lion	獅子	*szï-dz* siz-dz
lobster	洋蝦	*yang-hsia* yang-sheeah
monkey	猴子	*hou-dz* hou-dz (ou *as in* soul)
mouse	小老鼠	*hsiao lào shù* sheeow low shoo
mule	騾子	*lo-dz* loh-dz
owl	猫頭鷹	*mao-tou-ying* mow-tou-ying
ox	黃牛	*hwang-niu* hwang-new
oysters	牡蠣	*móu-li* mou-lee
parrot	鸚鵡	*ying wu* ying-woo
partridge	鷓鴣	*dje-gu* jeh-goo
pheasant	野雞	*yé-gi* yea-gee
pig	猪	*dju* joo
pike (sea-)	猴子魚	*hou-dz yü* hou-dz yeu
rat	老鼠	*láo-shú* low-shoo
salmon	狗頭魚	*góu-tou yü* gou-tou yeu
sea-fish	海魚	*hái-yü* hi-yeu
seal	海狗	*hai-góu* hi-gou

English	Chinese	Romanized Pronunciation
Sheep	羊	*yāng* yang
snipe	沙錐鳥	*[s]ha-djui niáo* shah-jway neeow
sole	比目魚	*bí-mùh yü* bee-moo yeu
sparrow	麻雀	*ma-chioh* mah-cheeoh
swallow	燕子	*yèn-dz* yen-dz
swan	天鵝	*tien-o* tee'en-oh
tiger	老虎	*láo-hú* low-hoo
trout	淡水魚	*dàn shúi yü* dan shway yeu
turkey	火雞	*hó-gi* hoh-gee
turtle	甲魚	*giah-yü* geeah-yeu
whale	鯨魚	*ging-yü* ging yeu

Insects and Reptiles

第五課　蟄物類

English	Chinese	Romanized Pronunciation
Ant	螞蟻	*má-i* mah-ee
bee	蜜蜂	*mìh-fung* mee-fung
beetle	甲蟲	*gìah-chung* geeah-chung
butterfly	蝴蝶	*hu-dìh* hoo-dee'eh

English	Chinese	*Romanized* Pronunciation
Caterpillar	毛蟲	*mao-chung* mow-chung
fly	蒼蠅	*tsang-ying* tsang-ying
frog	蝦蟆	*hsia-ma* sheeah-mah
gnat	蜹子	*rùì-dz* rway-dz
insect	蟲	*chung* chung
lizard	壁虎	*bìh-hú* bee-hoo
mosquito	蚊子	*wen-dz* wun-dz
silkworm	蠶	*tsān* tsan
snail	蝸牛	*wa-niu* wah-new
snake	蛇	*shē* sheh
spider	蜘蛛	*djï-dju* jirr-joo

Trees, Fruits, Flowers, and Vegetables

第六課　　植物類

English	Chinese	*Romanized* Pronunciation
Apple	蘋菓	*pin-go* pin-go
apricot	杏子	*hsìng-dz* shing-dz
ash	槐樹	*hwāi shù* hwi shoo
asparagus	龍鬚菜	*lung-sü-tsai* lung seu tsi

English	Chinese	*Romanized* Pronunciation
Beans	蠶荳	*tsan-dòu* tsan dou
beech-tree	椎樹	*chūi shù* chway shoo
beetroot	紅菜頭	*hung-tsai-tou* hung tsi tou
birch	樺樹	*hwà shù* hwah shoo
cabbage	包菜	*bao-tsai* bow tsi
carrot	胡蘿蔔	*hu-lo-bo* hoo lo bo
cauliflower	花椰菜	*hwa-no-tsai* hwah no tsi
celery	芹菜	*chin-tsai* chin tsi
cherry	櫻桃	*ying-tao* ying tow
cucumber	黃瓜	*hwang-gwa* hwang gwah
figs	無花果	*wu-hwa-go* woo hwah go
fir-tree	杉樹	*shan shù* shan shoo
grapes	葡萄	*pu-tao* poo tow
leaf	葉	*yèh* yeh
lemon	香櫞	*hsiang-yüen* sheeang yeuehn
lettuce	萵笋	*wo-swen* wo sun
lily	百合	*beh-hòh* beh ho
lime	檸檬	*ning-yüen* ning yeuehn
melon	瓜	*gwa* gwah
nut	白果	*beh-gó* beh go
oak-tree	橡樹	*hsiàng shù* sheeang shoo

English	Chinese	*Romanized* Pronunciation
Peach	桃子	*tao-dz* tow-dz
pear	梨	*li* lee
peas	豌荳	*wán-dòu* wan dou
pine (tree)	松樹	*sung shù* sung shoo
pineapple	菠蘿蜜	*bo-lo-mih* bo lo mee
plum	李子	*lí-dz* lee-dz
potatoes	山芋	*shan-yü* shan yeu
rose	月月紅	*yüeh-yüeh-hung* yeueh yeueh hung
spinach	菠菜	*bo-tsai* bo tsi
strawberry	楊梅	*yang-mei* yang may
tomato	番茄	*fan-chie* fan chee'eh
tree	樹	*shù* shoo
tulip	山慈菇	*shan-tsï-gu* shan tsz goo
turnip	蘿蔔	*lo-bo* lo-bo
vine (grape)	葡萄樹	*pu-tao shù* poo tow shoo
violet	紫羅蘭	*tsï-lo-lan* tsz lo lan
walnut	核桃	*hěh-tao* heh tow

Colours

第 七 課　　顏 色 類

English	Chinese	*Romanized* Pronunciation
Black	黑	*heh* heh
blue	藍	*lan* lan
brown	棕色	*dzung-sèh* dzung seh
crimson	胭脂	*yen-djĭ* yen jirr
dark	深色	*shen-sèh* shun seh
green	綠	*lòh* loo
grey	灰色	*hwei-sèh* whey seh
indigo	靛青	*dĭen ching* dee'en ching
light (pale)	淡色	*dàn-sèh* dan seh
orange	土紅色	*tu hung sèh* too hung seh
pink	水紅	*shúi-hung* shway hung
purple	紫	*tsĭ* tsz
red	紅	*hung* hung
scarlet	大紅	*dà-hung* dah hung
violet	蓮青	*lien-ching* lee'en ching
white	白	*beh* beh
yellow	黃	*hwang* hwang

Times and Seasons

第 八 課　　時 節 類

English	Chinese	*Romanized* Pronunciation
Afternoon	下晝	*hsia-djou* sheeah jou
Christmas	聖誕節	*shèng-dàn-dzieh* shun*g* dan jee'eh
dawn	黎明	*li-ming* lee ming
day	白日	*beh rëh* beh rirr
days of the week	禮拜的日	*lí-bài dy rih* leebī dee rirr
Sunday	主日	*dju-rïh* joo rirr
Monday	禮拜一	*lí-bài ìh* lee-bī ee
Tuesday	禮拜二	*lí-bài èr* lee-bī ur
Wednesday	禮拜三	*lí-bài san* lee-bī san
Thursday	禮拜四	*lí-bài szï* lee-bī siz
Friday	禮拜五	*lí-bài wu* lee-bī wu
Saturday	禮拜六	*lí-bài lùh* lee-bī loo
day-time	日間	*rìh-gien* rirr gee'en
Easter	復生節	*fùh-seng dzieh* foo-sun*g* jee'eh
evening	晚上	*wán-shàng* wan shang
every day	每日	*méi-rïh* may rirr
fortnight	兩禮拜	*liáng lí-bài* leeang lee-bī

English	Chinese	*Romanized* Pronunciation
Good-Friday	主死日	*dju szï rïh* joo siz rirr
holiday	放假日	*fàng gia rïh* fang geeah rirr
hour	一點鐘	*ìh dien djung* ee dee'en jung
—, half-an-	半點鐘	*bàn dien djung* ban dee'en jung
mid day, noon	正午	*djèng-wu* jung woo
midnight	半夜	*bàn-ye* ban yea
minute	一分鐘	*ìh fen djung* ee fun jung
Month	一個月	*ìh go yüeh* ee go yeueh
months (the)	十二月名	*shïh rï yüeh ming* shirr ur yeuch ming
January	正月	*djeng-yüeh* jung yeueh
February	二月	*èr-yüeh* ur yeueh
March	三月	*san-yüeh* san yeueh
April	四月	*szï-yüeh* siz yeueh
May	五月	*wú-yüeh* woo yeueh
June	六月	*lúh-yüeh* loo yeueh
July	七月	*tsih-yüeh* chee yeueh
August	八月	*bàh-yüeh* ba yeueh
September	九月	*giu-yüeh* geeoo yeueh
October	十月	*shïh-yüeh* shirr yeueh
November	十一月	*shïh-ìh yüeh* shirr ee yeueh
December	十二月	*shïh-èr yüeh* shirr ur yeueh

English	Chinese	Romanized Pronunciation
Morning	早上	*dzao-shàng* dzow shang
night	黑夜	*heh-ye* heh yea
quarter (3 months)	一季	*ìh-gi* ee gee
seasons, the four	四季	*szï-gee* siz gee
Spring	春季	*chwen-gi* chwun gee
Summer	夏季	*hsia-gi* sheea gee
Autumn	秋季	*chiu-gi* cheeoo gee
Winter	冬季	*dung-gi* dung gee
second	第二	*di-er* dee ur
sunrise	日出來	*rïh-chuh-lai* rirr choo lī
sunset	日落了	*rïh-lòh-liao* rirr lo liow
time	時候	*shï-hòu* shirr hou
to-day	今日	*gin-rïh* gin rirr
to-morrow	明天	*ming-tien* ming tee'en
— morning	明早	*ming-dzao* ming dzow
to-night	今晚	*gin-wán* gin wan
twilight	黃昏	*hwang-hwun* hwang hwun
week	一禮拜	*ìh li-bài* ee lee-bī
year	一年	*ìh nien* ee nee'en
yearly	每年	*měi nien* may nee'en
yesterday	昨天	*dzoh-tien* dzo tee'en

Town and Country

第九課　　城鄉類

English	Chinese	*Romanized* Pronunciation
Bridge	橋	*chiăo* cheeow
building (edifice)	房屋	*fang wuh* fang woo
bush	樹秧	*shù yang* shoo yang
country	鄉下	*hsiang-hsia* sheeang sheeah
ditch	溝	*gou* gou
farm	莊	*djwang* jwang
fence	籬笆	*li-ba* lee bah
field	田	*tiēn* tee'en
foot-path	小路	*hsiao lù* sheeow loo
forest	樹林	*shu-lin* shoo lin
gate	籬笆門	*li-ba mēn* lee-bah mun
grass	草	*tsáo* tsow
hay	乾草	*gan tsáo* gan tsow
hut	草房	*tsao-fang* tsow fang
inn	飯店	*fàn-dìen* fan dee'en
lane	山路	*shan lù* shan loo
market	菜市	*tsài-shï* tsĭ shirr
meadow	草地	*tsáo dì* tsow dee

English	Chinese	*Romanized* Pronunciation
mile	里	*lì* lee
mill-wheel	水磨輪	*shui-mo lwèn* shway mo lwun
monument	記念碑	*gì nìen pāi* gee nee'en pī
palace	宮殿	*gung-dien* gung dee'en
police-station	警察局	*gíng chāh gūh* ging cha geu
prison	監牢	*gien-lao* gee'en low (*like* now)
river	河	*hō* ho
road	道路	*dào-lu* dow loo
school	學堂	*hsioh-tang* sheeoh-tang
shepherd	牧羊的	*muh-yang dy* moo-yang dee
shop	店	*dìen* dee'en
street	街	*giai* geeī
town	鎮	*djèn* jun
valley	谷	*gúh* goo
village	村	*tswen* tswun
well, a	井	*djìng* jing
wood, a	樹林	*shù lĭn* shoo lin

Mankind: Relations

第十課　五倫類

English	Chinese	*Romanized* Pronunciation
Aunt	姑媽	*gu-ma* goo mah
boy	男孩子	*nān hai-dz* nan hi dz
brother	兄弟	*hsiung-dì* sheeung dee
brother-in-law	姊夫	*dzie-fu* jay foo
child	孩子	*hai-dz* hi-dz
cousin	表哥	*biao-go* beeow go
daughter	女兒	*nü-er* neu urr
daughter-in-law	媳婦	*sìh-fù* shee foo
family	全家	*tsüen gia* cheuehn geeah
father	父親	*fù-tsin* foo chin
father-in-law	丈人	*djàng-ren* jang run
girl	閨女	*gwei-nü* gway neu
granddaughter	孫女	*swen-nü* swun neu
grandfather	爺爺	*ye-ye* yea yea
grandmother	奶奶	*nai-nai* ni ni
grandson	孫子	*swen-dz* swun dz
husband	丈夫	*djàng-fu* jang foo
man	人	*rèn* run

English	Chinese	Romanized Pronunciation
marriage	嫁娶	*gìa-tsü* geeah tseu
mother	母親	*mú-tsin* moo chin
mother-in-law	丈母	*djàng-mu* jang moo
nephew	姪子	*djïh-dz* jirr-dz
niece	姪女	*djïh-nü* jirr-neu
parents	父母	*fù-mu* foo moo
relations	家屬	*gia-shuh* geeah shoo
sister (elder)	姊姊	*dzie-dzie* jeeay jeeay
— (younger)	妹妹	*mèi-mèi* may may
sister-in-law (elder)	姨子	*i-dz* ee-dz
— (younger)	姑子	*gu-dz* goo-dz
son	兒子	*er-dz* urr-dz
son-in-law	女壻	*nü-sü* neu seu
uncles	叔伯	*shuh-beh* shoo beh
widow	寡婦	*gwa-fù* gwa-foo
widower	鰥夫	*gwán-fu* gwan-foo
wife	妻子	*tsi-dz* chee-dze
woman	婦人	*fuh-ren* foo run

The Human Body

第十一課　　肢體類

English	Chinese	*Romanized* Pronunciation
Ankle	踝骨	*hwa-guh* hwah goo
arm	膊子	*bòh-dz* bo-dz
back	背	*bèi* bay
beard	鬍鬚	*hu-sü* hoo-seu
body	身體	*shen-ti* shun tee
bones	骨頭	*gùh-tóu* goo tou
bowels	腸子	*chang-dz* chang-dz
brain	腦子	*náo-dz* now-dz
breast, chest	胸膛	*hsiung-tang* sheeung tang
chin	下頦	*hsia-hai* sheeah hi
ear (external)	耳朵	*ér-dó* urr doh
elbow	肘子	*djóu-dz* jou-dz
eye	眼睛	*yén-dzing* yen jing
face	臉	*lién* lee'en
fingers	指頭	*djī-tou* jirr-tou
foot	脚	*giōh* geeoh
hair	頭髮	*tou-fàh* tou fa
hand	手	*shóu* shou

English	Chinese	Romanized Pronunciation
head	頭	*tŏu* tou
heart	心	*sin* sin
knee	膝蓋	*sih-gài* shee guy
leg	大腿	*dà-túi* dah tway
limbs (four)	四肢	*szï-djï* siz jirr
lips	嘴	*dzui* dsway
liver	肝	*gan* gan
lungs	肺	*fèi* fay
moustache	鬍子	*hu-dz* hoo-dz
mouth	口	*kóu* kou
neck	頸子	*ging-dz* ging-dz
nose	鼻子	*bi-dz* bee-dz
shoulders	肩膊	*gien-bóh* gee'en bo
side	脅	*hsïeh* shee'eh
skin	皮	*pï* pee
stomach	肚子	*du-dz* doo-dz
teeth	牙齒	*ya-chi* ya chirr
throat	喉嚨	*hou-lung* hou lung
thumb	大拇指	*dà-mú-djï* da-moo djirr

English	Chinese	*Romanized* Pronunciation
toe	脚趾	*gioh-djï* geeo jirr
tongue	舌頭	*shèh-tou* sheh tou
wrist	手腕	*shóu-wán* shou wan

Health

第十二課 衛生類

English	Chinese	*Romanized* Pronunciation
Ambulance	病人車	*bìng-ren che* bing run chay
bandage	裹紮布	*gó-chah bù* go cha boo
bite	咬	*yáo* yow
blind person (a)	瞎子	*hsiah-dz* sheea-dz
bruise	打傷處	*dá shang chù* dah shang choo
burn	燒傷處	*shao shang chù* show shang choo
chemist	藥商	*yòh shang* yo shang
chill	冷	*léng* lung
—, to catch a	傷風	*shang fung* shang fung
contagion	傳染病	*chwan-ran bìng* chwan ran bing
corns	鷄眼	*gi-yén* gee yen
cough	咳嗽	*kèh-sù* kessoo

English	Chinese	Romanized Pronunciation
cure, to	醫病	*i-bing* ee-bing
dentist	牙醫	*yā i* ya ee
diarrhœa	瀉病	*sìe bìng* sheeay bing
disease, illness	病	*bìng* bing
doctor	醫生	*i-seng* ee sung
doctor's fee	藥敬	*yòh gìng* yo ging
faint, to	暈倒	*hwèn dáo* hwun dow
fever	熱病	*rèh-bing* reh bing
fracture	斷骨	*dwàn gùh* dwan goo
gout	酒瘋病	*dzíu feng bìng* jeeoo fung bing
headache	頭痛	*tōu tùng* tou tung
hospital	醫院	*i-yüèn* ee yeuehn
ill, sick	作嘔	*dzòh óu* dzo ou
indigestion (temporary)	心口疼	*sin kóu teng* sin kou tung
— (chronic)	積食	*dzih shih* jee shirr
inflammation	熱腫	*rèh djúng* rêh jung
medicine	藥	*yòh* yo
ointment	膏藥	*gao-yoh* gow yo
pain	痛	*tùng* tung
pill	丸藥	*wan-yoh* wan yo
poison	毒藥	*dùh-yoh* doo yo

English	Chinese	Romanized Pronunciation
Poultice	敷藥	*fu yòh* foo yo
prescription	藥方	*yòh fang* yo fang
scald	燙	*tàng* tang
sea-sickness	暈船	*yün chwān* yeuin chwan
sore throat	喉痛	*hōu-tùng* hou tung
sprain	扭筋	*niú gin* new gin
tonic	補藥	*bú-yòh* boo yo
wound	刀傷處	*dao shang chù* dow shang choo

Food and Drink

第十三課　飲食類

English	Chinese	Romanized Pronunciation
Bacon	鹹肉	*hsien-rùh* shee'en roo
beef	牛肉	*niu rùh* new roo
beef-steak	鐵耙牛肉	*tiéh ba nīu rùh* tee'eh ba new roo
beer, ale	皮酒	*pī dziu* pee jeeoo
bottle	玻璃缾	*bo-li pīng* bo lee ping
bread	麵包	*mìen-bao* mee'en bow
—, brown	麩皮麵包	*fu pī mìen-bao* foo pee mee'en bow

English	Chinese	*Romanized* Pronunciation
Breakfast	早飯	*dzáo fàn* dzow fan
butter	牛奶油	*niu nái yū* new nī you
cake	蛋糕	*dàn-gao* dan gow (ow *as* now)
cheese	牛奶餅	*niu-nái bing* new nī bing
chocolate	啅科拉	*chọ̀h ko la* chokola
cigar	捲煙	*güén yen* geuehn yen
coffee	咖啡	*kà-fèi* kafay
cream	牛奶皮	*niu-nái pī* new nī pee
dinner	中飯	*djung fàn* djung fan
eggs (hen's)	鷄蛋	*gi-dàn* gee-dan
fat (meat)	肉油	*rùh-yu* roo you
flour	麵粉	*mièn-fén* mee'en fun
ham	火腿	*hó-túi* ho tway
jam	菓醬	*gó dziàng* go jeeang
lamb	羔羊肉	*gao-yang rùh* gow yang roo
lean meat	瘦肉	*sòu rùh* sou roo
fat meat	肥肉	*fei-rùh* fay roo
lemonade	荷蘭水	*ho-lan shúi* hoh lan shway
meat (cooked)	葷菜	*hwen-tsài* hwun tsī
milk	牛奶	*niu-nái* new nī
mustard	芥末	*giài-mòh* geeī mo

English	Chinese	*Romanized* Pronunciation
Mutton	羊肉	*yāng rùh* yang-roo
oil	油	*yū* yoo
onion	葱	*tsung* tsung
pepper	胡椒	*hu-dziao* hoo jeeow
pork	猪肉	*dju-rùh* joo roo
pudding	糕	*gao* gow
rice (plant)	稻子	*dào-dz* dow dz
— (grain)	米	*mí* mee
— (boiled)	飯	*fàn* fan
salad	生菜	*seng-tsài* sung-tsi
salt	鹽	*yēn* yen
sausage	香腸子	*hsiang-chang-dz* sheeang chang-dz
soda-water	炭酸水	*dàn-swan shúi* tansan shway
soup	湯	*tang* tang
sugar	白糖	*beh-tang* beh-tang
supper	晚飯	*wán fàn* wan fan
tea	茶	*chā* chah
tobacco	煙	*yen* yen
veal	小牛肉	*hsiáo nīu rùh* sheeow new roo
vegetables	菜蔬	*tsài sù* tsi soo
vinegar	醋	*tsù* tsoo

English	Chinese	*Romanized* Pronunciation
Water (boiled)	熟水	*shùh-shúi* shoo shway
wine	酒	*dzíu* jeeoo

Cooking and Eating Utensils

第十四課 器皿類

English	Chinese	*Romanized* Pronunciation
Basin	碗	*wán* wan
coffee-pot	咖啡壺	*kà-fèi hu* ka fay hoo
cruet-stand	作料架	*dzòh-liào gìa* dzo leeow geeah
cup	杯子	*bei-dz* bay dz
dish	器皿	*chì-míng* chee ming
fork	叉子	*cha-dz* chah dz
glass (tumbler)	玻璃杯	*bo-li bei* bo lee bay
kettle	水壺	*shúi-hu* shway hoo
knife	刀	*dao* dow
oven	爐子	*lu-dz* loo dz
plate	盆子	*pen-dz* pun-dz
saucepan, pot	罐子	*gwàn-dz* gwan dz
saucer	碟子	*dìeh-dz* dee'eh dz

English	Chinese	Romanized Pronunciation
Serviette	飯襠	*fàn-dang* fan dang
spoon	調羹	*tiao-geng* teeow gung
—, table-	大勺子	*dà shŏh-dz* dah sho-dz
—, tea-	小勺子	*hsiáo shŏh-dz* sheeow sho-dz
table-cloth	桌布	*djoh-bù* jo boo
tea-pot	茶壺	*cha-hu* chah hoo
tray	托盤	*tŏh-pan* to pan
wineglass	酒杯	*dzíu-bei* jeeoo bay

Dress and Dressing

第十五課　衣飾類

English	Chinese	Romanized Pronunciation
Bracelet	手鐲	*shóu-djoh* shou joh
braces	褲帶	*kù-dài* koo di
brooch	胸口針	*hsiung-kóu djen* sheeung kou jun
brush	刷子	*shwah-dz* shwa-dz
button	鈕扣	*niú-kòu* new kou
button-hook	扣鈕鈎子	*kòu níu gou-dz* kou new gou dz
calico	洋布	*yang-bù* yang boo

English	Chinese	Romanized Pronunciation
Cap	小帽	*hsiáo mào* sheeow mow (*like* now)
cloak, cape	披風	*pi fung* pee fung
clothes-brush	衣刷子	*i-shwah-dz* ee shwa-dz
coat	大衫	*dà shan* da shan
comb	梳子	*su-dz* soo dz
cotton	棉線	*mien-hsìen* mee'en shee'en
dress (lady's)	婦人衫	*fu-ren shan* foo run shan
dressing-gown	夜長衣	*yè chāng i* yea chang ee
evening-dress	禮服	*li-fùh* lee foo
flannel	法蘭絨	*fàh-lan rung* fa lan rung
flannelette	法蘭布	*fàh-lan bù* fa lan boo
gaiters	脚蓋	*gioh-gài* geeo guy
garters	襪帶	*wah-dài* wa di
gloves	手套	*shóu tào* shou tow (*like* now)
hair-pin	簪子	*dzan-dz* dzan-dz
hat	大帽	*dà-mào* da mow
jewellery	首飾	*shóu-shïh* shou shirr
lace	花邊	*hwa-bien* hwah bee'en
linen	細夏布	*hsì hsia bù* shee sheeah boo
muslin	洋紗	*yang-sha* yang shah
necktie	頸帶	*ging-dài* ging di

English	Chinese	*Romanized* Pronunciation
Needle	針	*djen* jun
overcoat	外褂	*wài-gwa* wī gwah
parasol	綢傘	*chou-sán* chou san
pins	大頭針	*dà tōu djen* da tou jun
pocket	口袋	*kóu-dài* kou dī
purse	錢匣子	*chien-giah-dz* chee'en geea-dz
rain-coat; water-proof	雨衣	*yü-i* yeu ee
razor	剃頭刀	*tì tōu tao* tee tou dow
ring	戒指	*giài-djï* geeī jirr
scissors	剪子	*dzién-dz* jee'en-dz
silk	綢子	*chou-dz* chou-dz
skirt	裙子	*chün-dz* cheun dz
soap	胰子	*i-dz* ee-dz
tooth-brush	牙刷	*ya-shwah* yah shwa
towel	手巾	*shóu-gin* shou-gin
trousers	褲子	*kù-dz* koo-dz
umbrella	雨傘	*yü-sán* yeu san
— (Japanese)	紙傘	*djï-sán* djirr san
watch	時表	*shï-biáo* shirr beeow
wool	絨線	*rung-hsien* rung shee'en

Washing List

第十六課　洗衣類

English	Chinese	Romanized Pronunciation
Aprons, pinafores	圍裙子	*wēi chün-dz* way cheun dz
bath-gowns	浴衣	*yüh-i* yeu ee
blankets	絨氈	*rung-tán* rung tan
bodices	女汗衫	*nú hàn shan* neu han shan
caps	帽子	*mào-dz* mow-dz
chemises	女襯衫	*nú chèn shan* neu chun shan
collars, linen	領子	*líng-dz* ling-dz
—, lace	花邊領	*hwa-bien ling* hwa-bee'en ling
coverlets	床氈	*chwang tán* chwang tan
cuffs	袖頭	*hsiù-tou* sheeoo-tou
drawers	襯褲子	*chèn-kù-dz* chun koo-dz
dresses, gowns	女長衫	*nú chāng shan* neu chang shan
flannel waistcoats	絨背心	*rūng bèi-sin* rung bay-sin
neckties	領帶	*ling-dai* ling di
night-dresses	夜衣	*yè-i* yea ee
petticoats	襯裙子	*djèn chün-dz* jun cheun dz
pillow-cases	枕頭套	*chén-tou tào* chun tou tow
pocket-handkerchiefs	手帕子	*shóu-pà-dz* shou pa dz

English	Chinese	*Romanized* Pronunciation
serviettes	飯襠	*fàn dang* fan dang
sheets	白床單	*beh chwang dán* beh chwang dan
shirts	汗衫	*hàn shan* han shan
sleeping-suit	睡衣	*shùi ì* shway ee
socks (pairs)	短襪子(雙數)	*dwán wàh-dz* dwan wa dz
stockings	長襪子	*chāng wàh-dz* chang wa dz
table-cloths	鋪桌布	*pu djoh-bù* poo jo boo
towels	手巾	*shóu gin* shou gin
under-vests	襯衫	*chèn shan* chun shan

House and Furniture

第十七課　家伙類

English	Chinese	*Romanized* Pronunciation
Arm-chair	擱手椅子	*gòh-shóu i-dz* go shou ee-dz
basket	籃子	*lan-dz* lan-dz
bed	床	*chwang* chwang
bedroom	臥房	*wò-fang* wo fang
bell	鐘	*djung* jung
blind	簾子	*lien-dz* lee'en dz

English	Chinese	*Romanized* Pronunciation
Book-case	書架	*shu-gìa* shoo geeah
box	箱子	*hsiang-dz* sheeang-dz
broom	掃箒	*sáo-djóu* sow jou (sow ***like*** now)
candle	蠟燭	*làh-djuh* la joo
candlestick	燭臺	*djuh-tai* joo-ti
carpet	毡條	*djan-tiao* jan teeow
ceiling	天花板	*tien-hwa bán* tee'en hwah ban
cellar	地窖	*dì-gào* dee gow
chair	椅子	*ì-dz* ee-dz
chest of drawers	衣櫃	*i-gwèi* ee gway
chimney	烟囪	*yen-chwang* yen chwang
clock	自鳴鐘	*dzì mīng djung* dz ming jung
closet (w.c.)	廁房	*szï-fang* siz fang
coal	煤炭	*mei-tàn* may tan
counterpane	被單	*bèi-dan* bay dan
cupboard	碗廚	*wán-chu* wan choo
curtains	帳子	*djàng-dz* jang-dz
cushion	褥子	*rùh-dz* roo-dz
dining-hall	飯堂	*fàn-tang* fan tang
dining-room	吃飯間	*chìh-fàn gien* chirr fan gee'en
door	門	*men* mun

English	Chinese	*Romanized* Pronunciation
Drawing-room	客堂	*kèh-tang* keh tang
electric light	電氣燈	*dìen-chi deng* dee'en chee dung
fender	火爐欄子	*hó-lu lan-dz* hoh loo lan-dz
floor	地板	*dì-bán* dee ban
garden	園子	*yüen-dz* yeuehn-dz
grate (fire-)	鐵爐底	*tìeh-lu dí* tee'eh loo dee
key	鑰匙	*yoh-chï* yo chirr
kitchen	廚房	*chu-fang* choo fang
lamp	燈	*deng* dung
larder	伙食房	*hó-shïh fang* ho shirr fang
library	書房	*shu-fang* shoo fang
light	光	*gwang* gwang
lock	鎖	*só* soh
looking-glass	鏡子	*gìng-dz* ging dz
matches	洋火	*yang-hó* yang hoh
passage	過道	*gò-dào* go dow
piano	八音琴	*bàh yin chin* ba yin chin
picture	畫	*hwà* hwah
pillow	枕頭	*djén-tou* jun tou
poker	火棍	*hó-gwèn* ho gwun
roof	屋頂	*uh-díng* woo ding

English	Chinese	Romanized Pronunciation
Room	房間	*fang-gien* fang gee'en
seat	座位	*dzò-wèi* dzoh way
sheets	單被	*dan-bèi* dan bay
shovel	鏟子	*chán-dz* chan-dz
sideboard	碗櫃	*wán-gwèi* wan gway
stairs	樓梯	*lou-ti* lou tee
steps	臺坡	*tai-po* tī poh
table	桌子	*djòh-dz* jo-dz
table-cloth	檯子布	*tai-dz bu* tī-dz boo
tiles (ornamental)	琉璃磚	*liu-li djwan* leeoo lee djwan
tiles (roof)	瓦	*ua* wah
tongs	鐵鉗	*tièh-chien* tee'eh chee'en
verandah	亮臺	*liang-tai* leeang tī
wall	牆	*chiang* cheeang
wardrobe	衣櫃	*i-gwèi* ee gway
window	窗戶	*chwang-hù* chwang-hoo

Religion

第十八課　宗教類

English	Chinese	*Romanized* Pronunciation
Almighty God	全能上帝	*chüen neng Shàng Dì* cheuehn nung Shangdee.
altar	祭壇	*dzì-tan* jee-tan
angel	天使	*tien-shï* tee'eń shirr
apostle	使徒	*shï-tu* shirr-too
baptise, to	施洗	*shï-hsi* shirr-shee
baptism	洗禮	*hsi-li* shee lee
believe, to	相信	*hsiang-hsìn* sheeang shin
believer	教友	*giào-yú* geeow yoo
bible	聖經	*shèng-ging* shung ging
Bible Society	聖書會	*shèng shu hwèi* shung shoo hway
burial	安葬	*an-dzàng* an dzang
cemetery	墳地	*fen-dì* fun dee
charity (love)	仁愛	*ren-ài* run i
Christian	基督徒	*Gi-dùh tu* Gee-doo too
Christianity	基督教	*Gi-dùh giào* Gee-doo geeow
church (believers)	教會	*giào-hwèi* geeow hway
clergyman	牧師	*mùh-szï* moo siz
Commandments, [the	誡命	*giài-mìng* geei ming

English	Chinese	*Romanized* Pronunciation
Communion	聖餐禮	*shèng-tsan lì* shung tsan lee
conscience	良心	*liang-hsin* leeang shin
conversion	感化	*gán-hwà* gan hwah
Creator, Maker	創造主	*chwang-dzao dju* chwang dzow joo
Cross, the	十字架	*shĭh-dzĭ gìa* shirr dz geeah
death	死亡	*szĭ-wang* siz-wang
devil	魔鬼	*mo-gwěi* moh gway
divine	教員	*giào-yüen* geeow yeuehn
duty	本分	*běn-fèn* bun fun
epistle	書信	*shu-hsìn* shoo shin
eternal, everlasting	永遠	*yúng-yüen* yung yeuehn
eternal life	永生	*yúng-seng* yung-sung
evil (*adj.*)	惡的	*òh-dy* o dee
evil (*n.*)	惡事	*òh-szĭ* o siz
faith	信心	*hsìn-hsin* shin shin
faithful (*adj.*)	篤信的	*dùh hsìn-dy* doo shin dee
forgive, to	赦免	*shè-mien* sheh mee'en
forgiveness	赦罪	*shè-dzùi* sheh dzway
glory	榮耀	*yung-yào* yung yow
God	上帝	*Shàng-dì* Shangdee
goodness	良善	*liang-shàn* leeang shan

English	Chinese	Romanized Pronunciation
Gospel	福音	*fùh-yin* foo yin
grace	恩典	*en-diĕn* un dee'en
happiness	福氣	*fùh-chì* foo chee
heart	心裏	*hsin-lí* shin lee
heaven	天堂	*tien-tang* tee'en tang
hell (Gehenna)	地獄	*dì-yüh* dee yeu
— (Hades)	陰間	*yin-gien* yin gee'en
holiness	聖潔	*shèng-gieh* shung gee'eh
holy spirit	聖靈	*shèng-ling* shung ling
hope	盼望	*pàng-wàng* pang wang
humility	謙虛	*chien-hsü* chee'en sheu
hymn	聖詩	*shèng shï* shung shirr
hymn-book	讚美詩書	*dzàn-méi shi shu* dzan may shirr shoo
immortality	永活	*yúng hòh* yung ho
infinite	無窮	*wu-chiung* woo cheeung
intercessor	中保	*djung-bào* jung bow
Jesus Christ	耶穌基督	*Yesu Gidùh* Yehsoo Geedoo
justice	公義	*gung-ì* gung ee
Kingdom of [Heaven	天國	*tien gwoh* tee'en gwoh
Lamb of God	上帝的羔羊	*Shangdi dy gao yăng* Shangdee dee gow yang
life	生命	*seng-ming* sung ming

English	Chinese	*Romanized* Pronunciation
Lord	主	*Dju* Djoo
Lord's Supper	聖餐	*shèng-tsan* shung t-an
love	愛	*ài* i
lust	淫慾	*yin yüh* yin yeu
mass (Christian)	彌撒	*mì-sàh* meesa
— (Buddhist)	打醮	*dá dzìao* dah jeeow
mediator	中保	*djung-báo* jung bow
meekness	溫柔	*wen-rou* wun rou
mercy	慈悲	*tsï-bei* tze bay
minister (verb)	服事	*fùh-szï* foo siz
miracle	神蹟	*shen dzih* shun jee
missionary	教士	*gìào-szï* geeow siz
morality	善德	*shàn dèh* shan deh
mortal	凡胎	*fan tai* fan ti
New Testament	新約	*hsin-yoh* shin yoh
obedience	順從	*shwen-tsung* shwun tsung
offertory	捐款	*güen-kwán* geuehn kuan
Old Testament	舊約	*gìu-yoh* geeoo yo
parable	比喻	*bi-yü* bee yeu
pardon	赦免	*she-mien* shay mee'en
peace	平安	*ping-an* ping an

English	Chinese	Romanized Pronunciation
Pity	憐憫	*lien-mín* lee'en min
praise	讚美	*dzan-méi* dzan may
prayer	禱告	*dáo-gào* dow gow
priest (Jewish)	祭司	*dzí-szï* jee siz
priest (Catholic)	神父	*shen-fù* shun foo
Protestant	基督敎徒	*Giduh giào tu* Geedoo geeow too
Protestantism	改新敎	*gái hsin giao* guy shin geeow
Providence	天道	*tien-dào* tee'en dow
pulpit	講臺	*giáng tái* geeang tī
purity	潔淨	*gieh-dzing* gee'eh jeeng
reconciliation	復和	*fùh-ho* foo-hoh
Redeemer	救世主	*giu-shï dju* geeoo shirr joo
redemption	救贖	*giu-shuh* geeoo shoo
religion	宗敎	*dzung giao* dzung geeow
repentance	痛悔	*tung-hwei* tung hway
resurrection	復生	*fùh-seng* foo sung
righteousness	義	*ì* ee
Roman Catholic	天主敎	*tien dju giao* tee'en joo geeow
Sabbath, the	主日	*dju rïh* joo rirr
sacrament	聖禮	*shèng li* shung lee
sacred	聖	*shèng* shung

English	Chinese	Romanized Pronunciation
Sacrifice	祭物	*dzi-wùh* jee woo
salvation	救法	*giu fàh* geeoo fa
Saviour, the	救主	*gìu dju* geeoo joo
Scripture, the	聖書	*shèng-shu* shung shoo
selfishness	私心	*szĭ hsin* siz shin
sermon	勸勉話	*chüen mien hwa* cheuehn mee'en hwah
service, divine	禮拜	*li-bài* lee bi
sin	罪愆	*dzui-chien* dzway chee'en
sinner	罪人	*dzui-ren* dzway run
Son of God	神的兒子	*shen-dy er-dz* shun dee ur dz
sorrow	憂愁	*yu-tsou* yoo tsou
soul	靈魂	*ling-hwen* ling hwun
Sunday school	主日學堂	*dju rĭh hsioh tang* joo rirr sheeo tang
temperance (general)	節制	*dzieh-djĭ* jee'eh jirr
temptation	試煉	*shĭ-lìen* shirr lee'en
thankfulness	感謝	*gan-sie* gan seeay
tract	勸世文	*chüen-shĭ wēn* cheuehn shirr wun
trust	信賴	*hsìn-lài* shin li
truth	眞理	*djen-li* jun lee
unbelief	不信	*bùh hsìn* boo shin
unfaithful	失信	*shĭh hsìn* shirr shin

English	Chinese	*Romanized* Pronunciation
Virtue	德行	*dèh-hsing* deh shing
wicked	邪的	*sie-dy* seeay dee
wickedness	兇惡	*hsiung-ðh* sheeung o
will	主意	*dju-ì* joo ee
wisdom	智慧	*djī-hwèi* jirr hway
Word of God	神的道	*shen dy dào* shun dee dow
world, the	世界	*shī-gìai* shirr geei
worship	敬拜	*gìng-bài* ging bi
worshipper	敬拜的	*gìng bài-dy* ging bi dee

Professions, Trades, &c.

第 十 九 課　　藝 術 類

English	Chinese	*Romanized* Pronunciation
Actor	戲班子	*hsi-ban-dz* shee ban-dz
actress	女旦	*nü-dàn* neu dan
architect	工程師	*gung-cheng-szī* gung chung siz
artist	美藝師	*méi ì szī* may ee siz
baker	作饅頭的	*dzðh man-tou dy* dzo man tou dee
banker	開銀行家	*kai yīn hāng gia* ki vin hang geeah

English	Chinese	*Romanized* Pronunciation
Barber	薙頭的	*tì tōu dy* tee tou dee
bookseller	賣書的	*mài shu dy* mī shoo dee
butcher	屠戶	*tu-hù* too hoo
carpenter	木匠	*mùh-dziang* moo jeeang
chemist (apothecary)	開藥店家	*kai yoh dìen gia* kī yo dee'en geeah
confectioner	製茶食的	*djï chā shïh dy* jirr cha shirr dee
cook	廚子	*chu-dz* choo-dz
dentist	牙醫生	*yā i-seng* yah ee-sung
doctor	博士	*boh-szï* bo siz
farmer	田戶	*tiēn hù* tee'en hoo
fisherman	漁人	*yü rēn* yeu run
fishmonger	魚商	*yü shang* yeu shang
florist	賣花的	*mài hwa dy* mī hwah dee
governess	女師	*nü szï* neu siz
greengrocer	賣菜的	*mài tsài dy* mī tsī dee
hairdresser (woman's)	絞臉的	*gíao lìen dy* geeow lee'en dee
hatter	作帽子的	*dzòh mào-dz dy* dzo mow-dz dee
jeweller	珠寶客	*dju-báo kèh* joo bow keh
lawyer	律師	*lüh szï* leu siz
maid-servant	使女	*shï nü* shirr neu
messenger	聽差的	*tìng chai dy* ting chī dee

English	Chinese	*Romanized* Pronunciation
money-changer	兌換銀錢的	*dùi-hwan yin-chien dy* dway hwan yin chee'en dee
nurse (female)	顧病婦	*gù bìng fù* goo bing foo
nurse (wet)	奶媽	*nái-ma* nī mah
optician	造眼鏡的	*dzào yěn-gìng dy* dzow yen ging dee
photographer	照像的	*djào hsìang dy* jow sheeang dee
physician	醫生	*i-seng* ee-sung
policeman	巡捕	*hsün-bú* sheun boo
porter (light)	看門的	*kan-men dy* kan mun dee
printer	印書的	*yìn shu dy* yin shoo dee
servant	用人	*yùng rēn* yung run
shoemaker	鞋匠	*hsiai dzìang* sheeī jeeang
shopkeeper	店主	*dìen djú* dee'en joo
singer	唱歌的	*chàng go dy* chang go dee
student	學生	*hsioh-seng* sheeo sung
surgeon	外科醫生	*wài ko i-seng* wī ko ee sung
surveyor	測量師	*tsèh lĭāng szī* tseh leeang siz
tailor	裁縫	*tsai-feng* tsī-fung
teacher	教習	*gìao-hsih* geeow shee
tradesman	匠人	*dziàng rēn* jeeang run
watchmaker	鐘表匠	*djung-bìao dziàng* jung beeow jeeang

Countries and Nations

第二十課　邦國類

English	Chinese	Romanized Pronunciation
Africa	亞非利加	*yàfeilìgia* yah fay lee geeah
America	亞美利加	*yàméilìgia* yah may lee geeah
American, an	美國人	*méi gwōh rēn* may gwo run
Asia	亞西亞	*yàsià* yah see yah
China	中國	*djung-gwoh* jung gwo
Chinaman, a	中國人	*djung-gwoh rēn* jung gwo run
England	英吉利	*yingìhlì* ying gee lee
English (language)	英國話	*ying gwoh hwa* ying gwo hwa
Englishman	英國人	*ying gwoh rēn* ying gwo run
Europe	歐羅巴	*ouloba* ou lo bah
France	法蘭西	*fàhlansi* fa lan see
Frenchman	法國人	*fàh-gwoh rēn* fa gwo run
Germany	德國	*dèh-gwoh* deh gwo
German, a	德國人	*deh-gwoh rēn* deh gwo run
Great Britain	大英國	*dà ying-gwoh* da ying gwo
India	印度	*yìn-dù* yin doo
Japan	日本	*rìh-bén* ribbun
Japanese, a	日本國人	*rìh-bén gwoh rēn* ribbun gwo run

English	Chinese	*Romanized* Pronunciation
Russia	俄國	*o-gwoh* oh gwo
Russian, a	俄國人	*o-gwoh rēn* oh gwo run
Scotland	蘇格蘭	*sukehlan* sookellan

Travelling

第二十一課　旅行類

English	Chinese	*Romanized* Pronunciation
Arrival	到	*dào* dow
bag	口袋	*kóu-dài* kou dī
— (hand)	手袋	*shóu-dai* shou dī
berth (on ship)	艙舖	*tsang-pu* tsang poo
bill (account)	清單	*ching-dan* ching dan
boarding-house	旅館	*lü-gwan* leu gwan
boat	船	*chwān* chwan
booking-office	售票房	*shòu piào fāng* shou peeow fang
box	箱子	*hsiang-dz* sheeang-dz
carriage, coach	馬車	*má-che* mah cheh
change (money)	兌換	*dùi-hwàn* dway hwan
charge (price)	價錢	*gìa-tsien* geeah chee'en

English	Chinese	Romanized Pronunciation
Class, first	頭等	*tǒudêng* tou dung
—, second	二等	*èr dêng* ur dung
—, third	三等	*sàn dêng* san dung
coachman	車夫	*che-fu* cheh foo
companion	同伴	*tung-bàn* tung ban
consul	領事官	*líng-szì gwan* ling siz gwan
cushion	椅墊	*ǐ-dièn* ee dee'en
custom-house	稅關	*shùi-gwan* shway-gwan
custom-house offi-[cer	稅吏	*shùi-li* shway lee
departure(by land)	起行	*chí hsīng* chee shing
— (by water)	上船	*shàng chwān* shang chwan
distance	遠離	*yüén lī* yeuehn lee
drive, a	坐馬車	*dzò má che* dzoh mah cheh
driver	車夫	*che-fu* cheh foo
dust (raised by wind)	灰塵	*chēn hwei* chun hway
duty	稅餉	*shùi hsiang* shway sheeang
duty-free	免稅	*mién shùi* mee'en shway
engine	汽機	*chì-gi* chee gee
— -driver	司機的	*szí gi dy* siz gee dee
expenses (trav.)	盤費	*pān fèi* pan fay
express (train)	快車	*kwài che* kwi cheh

English	Chinese	*Romanized* Pronunciation
Fare (charge)	水脚	*shúi gioh* shway geeoh
good-bye	一路平安	*ìh lù ping-an* ee loo ping ar
guard (railway)	車守	*che shóu* cheh shou
guidance	領路	*líng lù* ling loo
guide, a	領路的	*líng lù-dy* ling loo dee
guide-book	游客指南	*yū keh djī nān* yoo keh djirr nan
hotel, inn	客寓	*keh yü* keh yeu
inspector	監督	*gien-dùh* gee'en doo
interpreter	繙譯	*fan-ìh* fan ee
journey	行程	*hsīng chēng* shing chung
junction (railway)	接軌道	*dzieh gwéi dào* jee'eh gway dow
key	鑰匙	*yoh-chī* yo chirr
label (tag)	簽條	*chien-tiao* chee'en teeow
landlady	客寓主婦	*keh-yü djú fù* keh yeu joo foo
landlord (hotel)	客寓主人	*kèh-yü djú rēn* keh-yeu joo run
lavatory	洗手所	*hsí shóu só* shee shou so
luggage, baggage	行李	*hsing-lí* shing lee
— -van (rail.)	行李車	*hsing-lí che* shing lee cheh
match (for light)	洋火	*yang hó* yang hoh
money-changer	兌換銀錢的	*dùi-hwan yin chiēn dy* dway hwan yin chee'en dee
money, ready-	現錢	*hsien chiēn* shee'en chee'en

English	Chinese	*Romanized* Pronunciation
Newspaper	新聞報	*hsin wen bào* shin wun bow
office	局子	*güh-dz* geu dz
an official	官	*gwan* gwan
official (adj.)	官的	*gwan-dy* gwan dee
omnibus	公客馬車	*gung kèh má che* gung keh mah cheh
package	包袱	*bao-fùh* bow foo
party (pleasure-)	樂游會	*loh yū hwèi* lo yeeoo hway
passenger	行客	*hsing-keh* shing keh
passport	護照	*hù-djao* hoo jow
payment (to make)	會賬	*hwèi djàng* hway jang
pier	碼頭	*má-tōu* mah tou
pipe (tobacco-)	烟管	*yen gwǎn* yen gwan
policeman	巡捕	*hsün-bú* sheun boo
porter (rail.)	脚夫	*gioh-fu* geeoh foo
—(light)	挑夫	*tiao-fu* teeow foo
portmanteau	旅行皮夾	*lü hsing pi-giah* leu shing pee geeah
price (cost)	價錢	*gìa chīen* geeah chee'en
purse	錢袋	*chien-dài* chee'en di
railway	鐵路	*tìeh-lù* tee'eh loo
— -carriage	鐵路車	*tìeh-lù che* tee'eh loo cheh
receipt	收條	*shou-tiao* shou teeow

English	Chinese	Romanized Pronunciation
Restaurant	飯店	*fàn dìen* fan dee'en
road, way	道路	*dào lù* dow loo
rug	毯子	*tan-dz* tan dz
saddle	馬鞍	*má an* mah an
ship	海船	*hái chwān* hī chwan
station	火車站	*hó che djàn* ho cheh jan
station-master	站長	*djàn djáng* jan jang
steamer	火輪船	*hó lwēn chwān* ho lwun chwan
stirrup	踏鐙	*dah dèng* da dung
telescope	千里鏡	*chien lí gìng* chee'en lee ging
ticket	票子	*piao-dz* peeow dz
—, return	回票	*hwēi piào* hway peeow
time-table	時刻表	*shī-kèh biao* shirr keh beeow
tip (gratuity)	賞錢 (酒錢)	*sháng chiēn (dziú-chiēn)* shang chee'en (jeeoo [chee'en)
train (rail.)	火車	*hó che* ho cheh
tram (electric)	電車	*dìen che* dee'en cheh
traveller	游歷客	*yū lì keh* yeeoo lee keh
trunk	衣箱	*i-hsiang* ee sheeang
tunnel	隧道	*sùi dào* sway dow
waiter	堂倌	*tang-gwan* tang gwan
waiting-room	客房	*kèh fāng* keh fang

English	Chinese	*Romanized* Pronunciation
saloon	客廳	*keh ting* keh ting
voyage	航海	*hāng hái* hang hi

Ships and Shipping

第二十二課　船務類

English	Chinese	*Romanized* Pronunciation
Anchor	鐵錨	*tiéh-mao* tee'eh mow
berth (of ship)	灣船處	*wan chwān chù* wan chwan choo
berth (bed)	床鋪	*chwang-pú* chwang poo
boat (ship)	船	*chwān* chwan
bow	船頭	*chwān tōu* chwan tou
boy	細崽	*hsi-dzai* shee dzi
cabin	房艙	*fang-tsang* fang tsang
captain	船主	*chwān djú* chwan joo
compass	羅盤	*lo-pan* loh pan
crew	水手	*shúi-shóu* shway shou
deck	船面	*chwān mièn* chwan mee'en
flag	旗子	*chi-dz* chee-dz
helm (rudder)	船舵	*chwān dò* chwan doh

English	Chinese	Romanized Pronunciation
Landing-stage	碼頭	*má-tou* mah tou
life-buoy	救命圈	*gìu mìng chüen* geeoo ming cheuehn
light-house	燈塔	*deng-táh* dung ta
mast	船桅	*chwān wēi* chwan way
oar	槳	*dziáng* jeeang
pilot	領港師	*lìng giáng szī* ling geeang siz
port (harbour)	港口	*giáng-kóu* geeang kou
porthole	窗戶	*chwang-hu* chwang hoo
— (for gun)	砲眼	*pào yén* pow yen
purser	買辦	*mái-bàn* mi ban
rope	繩索	*shēng sóh* shung so
sail (a)	篷	*pēng* pung
sail (to)	行船	*hsīng chwān* shing chwan
seaman (sailor)	水手	*shúi-shóu* shway shou
sea-sickness	暈船病	*yùn chwān bìng* yeuin chwan bing
ship	海船	*hái chwān* hi chwan
steamboat	輪船	*lwēn chwān* lwun-chwan
steersman	舵工	*dò gung* doh gung
stern	船艄	*chwān shao* chwan show
steward	管事的	*gwán szī dy* gwan siz dee

Trade and Commerce

第二十三課　買賣類

English	Chinese	*Romanized* Pronunciation
Accept, to (bill)	收票	*shou pìao* shou peeow
acceptor	簽票人	*chien pìao rēn* chee'en peeow run
account	賬目	*djàng-mùh* jang moo
—, to close	結賬	*gieh djàng* gee'eh jang
—, to settle an	清賬	*ching djàng* ching jang
—, current	流水賬	*liū shúi djàng* leeoo shway jang
—, on joint	公共賬	*gung gùng djàng* gung gung jang
accountant	管賬師	*gwán djàng szï* gwan jang siz
address	住址	*dju-djï* joo jirr
advance (money)	墊款	*diĕn-kwán* dee'en kwan
advice, letter of	交銀信	*giao yīn sìn* geeow yin sin
affidavit	畫押約	*hwà yàh yŏh* hwah ya yo
after date	期後	*chi hŏu* chee hou
— sight	見後付	*gìen hŏu fù* gee'en hou foo
agent	經理人	*ging lí rēn* ging lee run
agreement	合同	*hoh-tung* ho tung
arrears	掛欠	*gwà-chìen* gwah chee'en
assets	貨物	*hŏ wuh* hoh woo

English	Chinese	*Romanized* Pronunciation
Assurance (guarantee)	擔保	*dan báo* dan bow
attorney (lawyer)	律師	*lü-szï* leu siz
auditor	查賬員	*cha djàng yüen* chah jang yeuehn
balance	存款	*tsun-kwan* tswun kwan
— -sheet	出入表	*chuh rùh biao* choo roo beeow
bank	銀行	*yin-hang* yin hang
banking	存銀	*tsūn yīn* tswun yin
bank-note	鈔票	*chào pìao* chow peeow
bankrupt	倒行東家	*dáo hāng dung-gia* dow hang dung-geeah
bankruptcy	倒行	*dáo hāng* dow hang
bearer	憑票	*pīng pìao* ping peeow
bill (accommodation)	欠單	*chìen-dan* chee'en dan
bill of exchange	匯票	*hwei-pìao* hway peeow
— of lading	提貨單	*tī hò dan* tee hoh dan
bond (security)	保單	*bào-dan* bow dan
book-keeper	司賬人	*szī djàng rēn* siz jang run
brokerage	掮客扣水	*gien kĕh kóu shúi* gee'en keh kow shway
business	生意	*seng-i* sung ee
buyer (customer)	買主	*mái djú* mi joo
cable address	電碼	*dìen má* dee'en mah
— -gram	水線電報	*shúi hsìen dìen bào* shway shee'en dee'en bow

English	Chinese	*Romanized* Pronunciation
Cable to	打電報	*dá dièn bào* dah dee'en bow
capital	本錢	*bén tsiēn* bun chee'en
cargo	貨物	*hò wuh* hoh woo
carriage (cost of)	水脚	*shúi-gioh* shway geeoh
carriage forward	請寄	*tsing gi* ching gee
carriage-paid	水脚付過	*shúi-gioh fù go* shway geeoh foo go
cash sale	現買	*hsien mài* shee'en mi
catalogue	目錄	*mùh-lùh* moo loo
chamber of commerce	商務總會	*shang wù dzúng hwèi* shang woo dzung hway
cheque, a	匯票	*hwèi-piào* hway peeow
cheque, crossed	匯劃票	*hwèi hwa piào* hway hwah peeow
clearing-house (customs)	稅關銀行	*shùi-gwan yin-hang* shway gwan yin hang
clerk	寫字人	*sie dzï rēn* say dz run
commerce	交易	*giao-ì* geeow ee
company, a joint-stock	合本公司	*hòh bén gung-szï* ho bun gung siz
—, a limited	有限公司	*yú hsièn gung-szï* yeeoo shee'en gung siz
consign, to	寄交	*gì giao* gee geeow
consignee	收交付的	*shou giao-fu dy* shou geeow foo dee
consignment	交付的物	*giao fù dy wuh* geeow foo dee woo
consignor	寄交的人	*gèe giao-dy rēn* gee geeow dee run
contra account	扣賬	*kòu djáng* kou jang

English	Chinese	*Romanized* Pronunciation
Contract, a	合同	*hòh-tung* ho tung
cost	價錢	*gìa-tsien* geeah chee'en
cost, insurance and freight (c.i.f.)	價錢水脚保險費	*gia-tsien shui-gioh bǎo-hsien fèi* geeah chee'en shway-geeoh bow shee'en fay
cost price	價値	*gìa-djïh* geeah jirr
credit balance	存款	*tswēn kwán* tswun kwan
creditor	債主	*djài djú* jĭ joo
customs duties	稅餉	*shùi-hsiang* shway sheeang
damages, compensation	壞貨物賠款	*hwài hò wuh pēi kwán* hwĭ hoh woo pay kwan
date, at three months	三個月期	*sàn gò yüèh chi* san go yeueh chee
debt	欠款	*chìen-kwán* chee'en kwan
debtor	債戶	*djài-hù* jĭ hoo
deliver, to	交送	*giao sùng* geeow sung
demurrage	貨物留輪船費	*hò wuh liū lwūn chwān fèi* hoh woo leeoo lwun chwan fay
directors	總辦	*dzúng-bàn* dzung ban
discount	折扣	*djeh kòu* jeh kou
—, to	打折扣	*dá djeh kòu* dah jeh kou
dividend	股息	*gú hsih* goo shee
dock	船塢	*chwān wú* chwan woo
dock and harbour dues	泊船費	*bèh chwān fèi* beh chwan fay
double entry	收支雙記法	*shou djī shwang gi fàh* shou jirr shwang gee fa

English	Chinese	Romanized Pronunciation
Draw, to (bill)	支銀	*djī yīn* jirr yin
drawee	應匯票人	*ying hwèi piào rēn* ying hway peeow run
drawer (of bill)	出匯票人	*chùh hwèi piao rēn* choo hway peeow run
duty	稅餉	*shùi hsiáng* shway sheeang
—, export	出口稅	*chùh kóu shùi* choo kou shway
—, import	進口稅	*dzìn kóu shùi* dzin kou shway
—, liable to	應完稅	*ying wan shùi* ying wan shway
— free	免稅	*miĕn shùi* mee'en shway
estimate, an	估價	*gú gia* goo geeah
exchange (monetary)	兌換	*dùi hwàn* dway hwan
export (-ation)	運出口	*yün chùh kóu* yeun choo kou
export, to	載出	*dzái chùh* dzi choo
exchange (market rate of)	市價,行情	*shï-gia ; hang-tsing* shirr geeah ; hang ching
firm, a	公司	*gung-szï* gung siz
free on board (f.o.b.)	免水脚	*miĕn shwui gioh* mee'en shway geeoh
freight (charge)	船運貨費	*chwān yün hò fèi* chwan yeun ho fay
— -ship	裝貨	*djwang hò* jwang hoh
goods	貨物	*ho-wuh* hoh woo
gross weight	連皮重	*liĕn pī djüng* lee'en pee jung
guarantee	保單	*báo dan* bow dan
guarantor	保人	*báo rēn* bow run

English	Chinese	Romanized Pronunciation
Holder (of bill)	執提貨單的	*djïh ti hò dan dy* jirr tee hoh dan dee
import	進口	*dzìn kóu* dzin kou
import, to	運貨進口	*yün hó dzìn kóu* yeun hoh dzin kou
import trade	進口生意	*dzìn kóu seng-ì* dzin kou sung ee
importer	運貨進口商	*yün hò dzìn kóu shang* yeuin hoh dzin kou shang
indemnity	賠款	*pei-kwán* pay kwan
indorse, to	簽字	*chien dzï* chee'en dz
indorsement	應付匯票的事	*yìng fù hwèi piào dy szï* ying foo hway peeow dee siz
indorsee	收應付匯票的人	*shou yìng fù hwèi piào dy rēn* shou ying foo hway peeow run
indorser	付滙票的人	*fù hwèi piào dy rēn* foo hway peeow dee run
instalment (of payment)	收價的一分	*shou gìa dy ih fèn* shou geeah dee ee fun
insurance company	保險公司	*báo hsien gung-szï* bow shee'en gung siz
—, fire	火險公司	*hó hsien gung-szi* hoh shee'en gung siz
—, marine	水險公司	*shúi hsien gung-szi* shway shee'en gung siz
— policy	保險單	*báo hsien dan* bow shee'en dan
— premium	保險費	*báo hsien fèi* bow shee'en fay
insure, to	保險	*báo hsien* bow shee'en
interest (rate of)	利息	*li-hsih* lee shee
invoice	開貨單	*kai hò dan* ki hoh dan
I.O.U.	欠票	*chìen piao* chee'en peeow

English	Chinese	*Romanized* Pronunciation
Landing charges	碼頭費	*má-tou-fèi* mah tou fay
liabilities	欠款	*chièn kwǎn* chee'en kwan
lighterage	駁船費	*bŏh chwān fèi* bo chwan fay
liquidation (wind-[up])	倒店賠款	*dáo dièn pei kwǎn* dow dee'en pay kwan
load, to	裝貨	*djwang hò* jwang ho
loss	虧本	*kweī bĕn* kway bun
mail-day	寄信日	*gì hsin rìh* gee shin rirr
manufacture, to	製造	*djì-dzao* jirr dzow
manufactured goods	製造物件	*dji-dzao wuh-gien* jirr dzow woo jee'en
manufacturer	製造廠主	*djì-dzao chǎng djú* jirr dzow chang joo
market (for goods)	貨市	*hò shì* hoh shirr
— -price	市價	*shì gia* shirr geeah
— -place	買賣市場	*mǎi mài shì chǎng* mi mi shirr chang
merchandise	商品	*shang pin* shang pin
merchant	商家	*shang gia* shang geeah
merchant ship	商船	*shang chwān* shang chwan
money	錢幣	*chiēn bì* chee'en bee
money-market	錢市	*chiēn shì* chee'en shirr
negotiable	通用票	*tung yùng piào* tung yung peeow
negotiate, to (business)	作交易	*dzoh giao-ì* dzo geeow ee
net cost	實價	*shĭh già* shirr geeah

English	Chinese	Romanized Pronunciation
Net profit	淨利	*dzìng-li* jing lee
— weight	淨重	*dzing djùng* jing jung
obligation (debt)	欠債	*chìen djài* chee'en ji
order, an	貨單	*hò dan* hoh dan
—, to	開貨單	*kai hò dan* ki hoh dan
package (case)	裝箱	*djwang hsiang* jwang sheeang
packing	襯箱物件	*chèn hsiang wuh gièn* chun sheeang woo gee'en
paid	交付了	*giao fù liáo* geeow foo leeow
par	平價	*pīng già* ping geeah
— of exchange	平價的買賣	*pīng già dy mái mài* ping geeah dee mi mi
partner	股東家	*gú-dung gia* goo dung geeah
partnership	合股商業	*hòh gú shang yèh* ho goo shang yeh
payable at date	到期付銀	*dào chi fù yīn* dow chee foo yin
payee	收銀的	*shou yīn dy* shou yin dee
payment	付銀	*fù yīn* foo yin
per annum	每年	*méi nìen* may nee'en
per cent., 2½	每年二分半息	*méi nìen èr fen bàn hsih* may nee'en ur fun ban shee
— —, 3	每年三分息	*méi nìen san fen hsih* may nee'en san fun shee
port of delivery	交貨碼頭	*giao hò ma-tou* jeeow ho ma-tou
port dues	入口稅	*ruh kóu shúi* roo kou shway
price, cost-	價目	*già muh* jeeah moo

English	Chinese	Romanized Pronunciation
Price list	價目單	*gia muh dan* jeeah moo dan
price, selling	賣價	*mái gìa* mi geeah
—, trade	行價	*hāng gìa* hang geeah
—, wholesale	批發價	*pi fah gìa* pee fa geeah
proceeds	貨價	*hò gìa* hoh geeah
profit	利息	*li-hsih* lee shee
—and loss account	利息虧折賬	*li-hsih kwei djĕh djang* lee shee kway jeh jang
promissory note	期票	*chi piào* chee peeow
prospectus	傳單	*chwān dan* chwan dan
punctual	照期的	*djào chi dy* jow chee dee
purchase, to	辦貨	*bàn hò* ban hoh
quality (of goods)	物品	*wùh pin* woo pin
quantity	幾多	*gi do* gee doh
quarter (3 months)	一季	*ih gì* ee gee
quotation (of price)	時價	*shī gìa* shirr geeah
quote, to	開價錢	*kai gìa chien* ki geeah chee'en
rate of exchange	金銀市價	*gin yin shī gìa* gin yin shirr geeah
receipts	進款	*dzìn kwán* dzin kwan
receipt	收條	*shou tiāo* shou teeow
reduction	減少	*gièn sháo* gee'en show (ow *as in* now)
re-export	再運出口	*dzài yün chuh kóu* dzi yeun choo kou

English	Chinese	Romanized Pronunciation
References	薦書	*dziȅn shu* jee'en shoo
register, to (letter)	掛號	*gwà hào* gwah how
registered letter	掛號信	*gwà hào hsìn* gwah how shin
registration	登册	*deng tsèh* dung tseh
— fee	登册費	*deng tsèh fei* dung tseh fay
remittance (a)	滙銀信	*hwèi yin hsìn* hway yin shin
rent	租金	*dzu gin* dzoo gin
reply	回信	*hwĕi hsìn* hway shin
—, to	作復	*dzoh fùh* dzo foo
representative	代表	*dài biao* di beeow
retail	小買賣	*hsiào mái mài* sheeow mi mi
—, to	作小買賣	*dzoh hsiáo mái mài* dzo sheeow mi mi
salary	薪水	*hsin shúi* shin shway
sale	出賣	*chuh mài* choo mi
salesman (seller)	店夥，賣貨的	*dièn hó (mài hó dy)* dee'en hoh (Mi hoh dee)
sample	貨樣	*hò yàng* hoh yang
security(guarantee)	保單	*báo dan* bow dan
sell, to	賣	*mài* mi
settling days	結算日	*gieh swàn rĭh* gieh swan rirr
shareholder	股東	*gú-dung* goo dung
shares	股分	*gú fèn* goo fun

English	Chinese	Romanized Pronunciation
Shares, preference	優先股	*yu sien gú* yeeoo see'en goo
—, railway	鐵路股	*tiéh-lù gú* tee'eh loo goo
shipping charges	船費	*chwān fèi* chwan fay
shipping house	船局	*chwān gŭh* chwan geu
shipping trade	船業	*chwān yèh* chwan yeh
solvent	本足商家	*bén dzŭh shang gia* bun dzoo shang geeah
stock (goods)	貨物	*hò wùh* ho woo
stock (shares, etc.)	股分	*gú fèn* goo fun
stock-broker	股分掮客	*gú fèn gien kĕh* goo fun gee'en keh
stock exchange	股分所	*gú fèn só* goo fun so
stock-taking	查驗存貨	*chā yén tswēn hò* chah yen tswun ho
stowage	裝載	*djwang dzài* jwang dzi
tare	減重	*gién djùng* gee'en djung
tariff (duties)	稅貨表	*shùi hò biáo* shway ho beeow
telegraphic address	電碼	*dìen má* dee'en mah
— code	電例	*dìen lì* dee'en lee
— remittance	電報滙銀	*dìen bào hwèi yin* dee'en bow hway yin
telephone	得律風	*delüfung* deh-leu-fung
— exchange	得律風公司	*dĕh lüh fung gung-szī* deh-leu-fung gung siz
— number	得律風號碼	*dĕh lüh fung hào má* deh-leu-fung how mah
tender, to	付欠款	*fù chìen kwán* foo chee'en kwan

English	Chinese	Romanized Pronunciation
Terms (conditions)	約條	*yoh tiāo* yoh teeow
tonnage	噸數	*dwen sù (shu)* dun soo (Shoo
— (dues)	噸費	*dwen fèi* dun fay
towing charges	拖船費	*to chwān fèi* toh chwan fay
trade	商務	*shang wù* shang woo
trade-mark	商標	*shang biao* shang beeow
transaction	貿易	*mào ì* mow ee
transfer	轉買	*djwàn mǎi* jwan mi
—, to	轉交	*djwàn giao* jwan geeow
traveller (commercial)	水客	*shúi keh* shway keh
underwriter	保險商	*bǎo hsièn shang* bow shee'en shang
unloading	提貨	*tī hò* tee hoh
value	價值	*gia djih* geeah djirr
vessel (ship)	商船	*shang chwān* shang chwan
voucher	憑單	*pīng dan* ping dan
warehouse	貨棧	*hò djàn* hoh jan
warranty	保單	*bǎo dan* bow dan
weight	分量	*fèn liāng* fun leeang
wharf	碼頭	*mǎ tōu* ma tou
wharfage	碼頭費	*mǎ tōu fèi* ma tou fay
wholesale	批發	*pī fah* pee fa

English	Chinese	*Romanized* Pronunciation
Wholesale merchant	批發商家	*pī fah shang gia* pee fa shang jeeah
winding-up	結完了	*giĕh wān liáo* gee'eh wan leeow

Correspondence

第二十四課　通信類

English	Chinese	*Romanized* Pronunciation
Address	住址	*djù djï* joo djirr
address, to	開住址	*kai djù djï* ki joo jirr
blotting-paper	墨水紙	*mèh shúi djï* meh shway jirr
date	日期	*rïh chi* rirr chee
envelope	信封	*hsìn feng* shin fung
ink	墨水	*mèh shui* meh shway
inkstand	墨水餅架	*mèh shúi pīng già* meh shway ping geeah
letter, note	短信	*dwán hsìn* dwan shin
— -box	信箱	*hsìn siang* shin sheeang
note-paper	信紙	*shìn djï* shin jirr
pen, steel (nib)	鋼筆頭	*gang bĭh tōu* gang bee tou
—, fountain	自來水筆	*dzï lāi shúi bĭh* dziz li shway bee
— -holder	筆杆	*bĭh gan* bee gan

English	Chinese	*Romanized* Pronunciation
Pencil	鉛筆	*chiēn bĭh* chee'en bee
penknife	削筆刀	*hsiŏh bĭh dao* sheeoh bee dow
seal	圖章	*tū djang* too jang
sealing wax	火漆	*hŏ tsih* hoh chee
sheet of paper, a	一張紙	*ih djang djĭ* ee jang jirr
signature	名號	*mīng hào* ming how
write, to	寫	*hsiĕ* sheeay
writing	文字	*wēn dzì* wun dz
— -desk	寫字桌	*hsiĕ dzì djoh* sheeay dz jo

Post office Telegraph and Telephone

第二十五課 郵傳類

English	Chinese	*Romanized* Pronunciation
Book post	寄書籍	*gì shu dzīh* gee shoo jee
destination	送往處	*sùng wáng chù* sung wang choo
excess (postage)	郵票不足之費	*yū piao bŭh dzŭh djī fèi* yoo peeow boo dzoo jirr fay
letter post	信件	*hsìn gièn* shin gee'en
money order	郵政滙票	*yū djèng hwèi piao* yoo jeeng hway peeow
newspaper wrapper	新聞紙包	*hsin wēn djĭ bao* shin wun jirr bow

English	Chinese	*Romanized* Pronunciation
Number (of order)	票子號頭	*piào-dz hào tōu* peeow dz how tou
parcel post	寄包件	*gì bao gìen* gee bow gee'en
postage stamp	郵票	*yū piào* yeeoo peeow
post-card	明信片	*mīng hsìn pìen* ming shin pee'en
poste-restante	存信處	*tswēn hsìn chù* tswun shin choo
postman	信差	*hsìn chai* shin chi
postmaster	郵政司	*yū djèng szī* yeeoo jung siz
post-office	郵政局	*yu djèng gūh* yeeoo jung geu
post-paid	郵費先付的	*yu fèi hsien fù dy* yeeoo fay shee'en foo dee
prepay, to	先付	*hsien fù* shee'en foo
register, to (a letter)	掛號	*gwà hào* gwah how
registered letter	掛號信	*gwà hào hsìn* gwah how shin
reply paid	回信資先付	*hwēi hsìn dzī hsien fù* hway shin dz shee'en foo
ring up, to	搖鈴得律風	*yao līng dĕh lüh fung* yow ling deh leu fung
telegram	電報	*dìen bào* dee'en bow
—, cost of	電費	*dìen fèi* dee'en fay
telegraph form	電報單	*dìen bào dan* dee'en bow dan
— messenger	電差	*dìen chai* dee'en chi
— office	電報局	*dìen bào gūh* dee'en bow geu
telegraph, to	打電報	*dá dìen bào* dah dee'en bow
telephone	得律風	*dēh lüh fung* deh leu fung

English	Chinese	*Romanized* Pronunciation
Telephone, to	打得律風	*dá dĕh lüh fung* dah deh leu fung
— call office	得律風公司	*dĕh lüh fung gung-szĭ* deh leu fung gung siz
— number	得律風號碼	*dĕh lüh fung hào má* deh leu fung how mah
weight	分量	*fèn lìang* fun leeang
—, over	過分量	*go fèn lìang* go fun leeang

Army and Navy

第二十六課　軍界類

English	Chinese	*Romanized* Pronunciation
Adjutant	翼長	*ì djáng* ee jang
— -general	副都統	*fu dù túng* foo doo tung
admiral	海軍中將	*hái gün djung dziang* hi jeun jung jeeang
admiral of fleet	海軍上將	*hai gün shang dziang* hi jeun shang jeeang
advance, to	前進	*chiēn dzìn* chee'en jin
aide-de-camp	中軍	*djung gün* jung jeun
alarm, an	驚報	*ging bào* ging bow
ammunition	軍火	*gün hó* jeun hoh
— (small arms)	手鎗軍火	*shóu chiang gün hó* shou cheeang jeun hoh
ammunition wagon	軍火車	*gün hó che* jeun ho che
anchor	鐵錨	*tiĕn māo* tee'eh mow

English	Chinese	*Romanized* Pronunciation
Anchorage	抛錨處	*pao māo chù* pow mow choo
armistice	停戰	*tíng djàn* ting jan
armour (mens')	盔甲	*kwei giáh* kway geeah
armour (ship's)	鐵板	*tiĕh bán* te'eeh ban
arms	軍械	*gün giài* jeun geei
arms, small	刺刀	*tsĭ dao* tsz dow
army	全軍	*tsüen gün* cheuehn jeun
army-corps	大軍	*dà gün* dah jeun
Army list	陸軍官級表	*luh gün gwan gih biao* loo jeun gwan gee peeow
— Medical Corps	衛生隊	*wèi seng dùi* way sung dway
army orders	號令	*hào lìng* how ling
artillery (guns)	大礮	*dà pào* dah pow
artillerymen	礮兵	*pào ping* pow bing
attack, an	攻擊	*gung gih* gung jee
—, frontal	迎面攻擊	*yīng mièn gung gih* ying mee'en gung jee
attack, to	進攻	*dzìn gung* jin gung
attention!	立正	*lih-djeng* lee jung
axe	斧頭	*fu tōu* foo tou
band	軍樂隊	*gün yòh dùi* jeun yo dway
band-master	軍樂長	*gün yòh djàng* jeun yo jang
bandsman	軍樂手	*gün yòh shóu* jeun yo shou

English	Chinese	*Romanized* Pronunciation
Barracks	兵房	*bing fāng* bing fang
barrel (rifle)	來福鎗管	*lāi fūh chiang gwàn* lī foo cheeang gwan
battalion	大隊步兵	*dà dùi bú bing* dah dway boo bing
battery	礮臺	*páo-tāi* pow tī
battle	交戰	*giao djan* geeow jan
battle-ship	戰船	*djàn chwan* jan chwan
bayonet	刺刀	*tsï dao* tsz dow
bayonets! fix-	上刺刀	*sháng tsï dao* shang tsz dow
bearer company	工兵	*gung bing* gung bing
bivouac, to	巡夜	*hsün ye* sheun yea
block (ship's)	船轆轤	*chwān lùh lu* chwan loo loo
blockade	封港	*feng giáng* fung geeang
bomb, -shell	炸彈	*djāh dàn* ja dan
bombard, to	放礮攻敵	*fàng páo gung dīh* fang pow gung dee
breastwork	營壘	*yīng lúi* ying lway
breech (of gun)	礮後膛	*páo hòu tāng* pow hou tang
breech-loader (rifle)	後膛鎗	*hòu tāng chiang* hou tang cheeang
bridle	馬嚼口	*ma dziōh kóu* ma jeeo kou
brigade	一旅	*ih lü* ee leu
brigadier-general	總兵	*dzung bing* dzung bing
bugle	號筒	*hào-tung* how tung

English	Chinese	Romanized Pronunciation
Bugler	號手	*hào shóu* how shou
bullet (rifle)	鎗子	*chiang dzï* cheeang dz
burst, to (shell)	炸裂	*djăh lièh* ja lee'eh
cable (anchor)	錨纜	*māo lán* mow lan
camp	營盤	*yïng-pān* ying pan
campaign	戰役	*djàn yìh* jan yee
camping ground	營地	*ying dì* ying dee
cannon, gun	大礮	*dà pào* dah pow
captain (army)	都司	*du-szï* doo siz
— (navy)	管帶	*gwàn dài* gwan di
capture, to (a ship)	擄獲船	*lú hòh chwān* loo ho chwan
cartridge	火藥包子	*hó yòh bao-dzï* ho yo bow dz
cartridge-pouch	火藥包子袋	*hò yòh báo-dz dài* ho yo bow dz di
casualties	死傷數	*sżï shang shù* siz shang shoo
cavalry	馬軍	*má gün* mah jeun
cease fire, to	停鎗	*ting chiang* ting cheeang
certificate, leave	准假執照	*djwen già djïh-djào* jwun geeah jirr jow
chain, anchor-	鐵鏈	*tièh lien* tee'eh lee'en
change step!	換步	*hwàn bù* hwan boo
chaplain (army)	軍營牧師	*gün yïng mùh szï* jeun ying moo siz
chaplain (navy)	兵艦牧師	*bing hsìen mùh-szï* bing shee'en moo siz

English	Chinese	*Romanized* Pronunciation
Charge!	衝鋒	*chung jeng* chung fung
chief-of-the-staff	參謀長	*tsan mōu djàng* tsan mou jang
colonel	參將	*tsan dziang* tsan jeeang
colours, the	旗子	*chī-dz* chee dz
column	一排兵	*ih pāi bing* ee pī bing
combatant	戰士	*djàn szï* jan siz
—, non-	戰外的	*djàn wài dy* jan wī dee
command, a	統領的職	*túng-líng dy djïh* tung ling dee jirr
—, to	統領三軍	*túng-lìng san gün* tung ling san jeun
commander (navy)	水師副管帶	*shúi-szī fù gwàn dai* shway siz foo gwan dī
— -in-chief	元帥	*yüēn-shùai* yeuehn shwī
commanding officer	統領	*túng-líng* tung ling
commissariat	軍糧局	*gün liāng güh* jeun leeang geu
company	一隊兵	*ih dùi bing* ee dway bing
company (artillery)	礮隊	*pào dùi* pow dway
—, half	半隊	*bàn dùi* ban dway
compass (mariner's)	羅盤	*lō-pān* loh pan
corporal	伍長	*wu-djáng* woo jang
correspondents	訪事人	*fáng szï rēn* fang siz run
court-martial	軍法裁判	*gün fah tsai pàn* jeun fah tsī pan
crew	船水手	*chwān shŭi shóu* chwan shway shou

English	Chinese	Romanized Pronunciation
Cruiser	巡洋艦	*hsün yāng hsien* sheun yang shee'en
cut (wound)	損傷	*swěn shang* sun shang
defaulter	違令人	*wēi lìng rēn* way ling run
defaulter's drill	違令操演	*wēi lìng tsao yěn* way ling tsow yen
defence	防守	*fāng shóu* fang shou
depot	招募部	*djao mò bù* jow mo boo
deserter	逃勇	*tāo yúng* tow yung
detachment	分隊	*fen dùi* fun dway
discipline	軍規	*gün gwei* jeun gway
disembark, to	登岸	*deng àn* dung an
dismount!	下馬	*hsía má* sheeah mah
division (of ships)	戰艦分隊	*djàn hsièn fen dùi* jan shee'en fun dway
division (army)	軍旅	*gün lü* jeun leu
doctor, the	醫生	*i-seng* ee sung
dress!	整隊	*djéng dùi* jung dway
drill	操演	*tsao yěn* tsow yen
drill-book	操法書	*tsao fàh shu* tsow fa shoo
driver	馬夫	*má-fu* mah foo
drum	鼓	*gú* goo
drummer	鼓手	*góo shóu* goo shou
duties	責任	*dzeh-rèn* dzeh run

English	Chinese	*Romanized* Pronunciation
Duty, guard	防守責任	*fāng shóu dzeh rèn* fang shou dzeh run
— outpost	外哨責任	*wài shao dzeh rèn* wī show dzeh run
dynamite	炸藥	*djah yoh* jah yo
embark, to	登船	*deng chwān* dung chwan
embarkation	登船的事	*deng chwān dy sżì* dung chwan dee siz
encampment	營盤	*ying-pān* ying pan
enemy	敵軍	*dìh-gün* dee jeun
enemy's position	敵軍的形勢	*dìh gün dy hsīng shì* dee jeun dee shing shirr
engagement	戰事	*djàn szì* jan siz
engineer (naval)	管輪	*gwán lwēn* gwan lwun
engineers (corps)	軍事工師	*gün szì gung szī* jeun siz gung siz
equipment	軍需	*gün hsü* jeun sheu
escort	護送兵	*hù sùng bing* hoo sung bing
exercise, bayonet	操刺刀	*tsao tši dao* tsow tsz dow
expedition	遠征隊	*yüen djeng dui* yeuehn jung dway
extend!	散開	*sàn kāi* san kī
eyes right, dress!	向前看齊	*hsiàng chien kàn tsı* sheeang chee'en kan chee
— left!	向左看	*hsiàng dzo kàn* sheeang dzoh kan
"fall in," to	合隊	*hōh dùi* ho dway
farrier	獸醫	*shòu-i* shou ee
fatigue (barrack)	營盤內事務	*ying-pān nùi szì wù* ying-pan nway siz woo

English	Chinese	Romanized Pronunciation
Field artillery	野礮隊	*yé pào dùi* yea pow dway
— exercises	操野操	*tsao ýe tsao* tsow yea tsow
— -glass	千里鏡	*chien lí gìng* chee'en lee ging
— -gun	車礮	*che pào* cheh pow
— -hospital	軍醫院	*gün-i yüen* jeun ee yeuehn
— -marshal	上將	*shang dziang* shang jeeang
— telegraph	軍電	*gün diěn* jeun dee'en
file (of men)	梯隊	*ti dùi* tee dway
fire!	放	*fàng* fang
fire, to	放礮	*fàng pào* fang pow
flag	旗幟	*chī djǐh* chee jirr
flank	翼隊	*ì dùi* ee dway
—, left	左翼隊	*dzo ì dùi* dzoh ee dway
—, righ	右翼隊	*yù ì dùi* yeeoo ee dway
fleet, the	艦隊	*hsien dui* shee'en dway
oot-soldier	步兵	*bù bing* boo bing
forage	馬料	*ma lìao* mah leeow
foresight (of rifle)	快鎗準	*kwài chiang djwěn* kwi cheeang djwun
formation	排列	*pāi lièh* pi lee'eh
fortress	礮臺	*pào-tāi* pow ti
forward!	向前	*hsiàng chien* sheeang chee'en

Eng	Chinese	*Romanized* Pronunciation
Front, the	隊前	*dùi chīen* dway chee'en
furlough	告假	*gào gía* gow jeeah
gallop, to	飛跑	*fei páo* fay pow
garrison	守備兵	*shóu bèi bing* shou bay bing
general, a	將軍	*dziang gün* jeeang geun
general officer	標統	*biao tùng* beeow tung
governor (military)	礮臺管帶	*pào-tai gwan dài* pow ti gwan di
ground, parade-	操場	*tsao chang* tsow chang
guard, the	衞隊	*wei dùi* way dway
—, advanced	前衞隊	*chīen wèi dui* chee'en way dway
—, rear-	後衞隊	*hòu wèi dùi* hou way dway
guard-room	卡子	*chìa-dz* cheeah dz
guard, to mount	上班	*sháng ban* shang ban
guard turn out!	換班	*hwán ban* hwan ban
gun, cannon	大礮	*dà pào* dah pow
gun-carriage	礮車	*pào che* pow cheh
gunner	礮手	*pào shóu* pow shou
gunpowder	火藥	*hó yòh* ho yo
halt!	立定	*lih ding* lee ding
hay (fodder	乾馬料	*gan má lìao* gan mah leeow
head-quarte	首營	*shóu yiñg* shou ying

English	Chinese	*Romanized* Pronunciation.
Horse-brush	馬刷箒	*ma shwah djou* mah shwa jou
— -cloth	馬衣	*má i* mah ee
— -shoe	馬脚鐵	*má gioh tièh* mah geeoh tee'eh
hospital, station-	軍醫所	*gün i só* jeun ee so
hospital-ship	軍醫船	*gün i chwān* jeun ee chwan
hut	草房	*tsáo fang* tsow fang
independent firing	各自放鎗	*gòh dzī fàng chiang* go dz fang cheeang
infantry	步兵	*bù bing* boo bing
—, mounted	騎馬步兵	*chī má bù bing* chee mah boo bing
inspection	閱校	*yüeh chiào* yeueh geeow
instructor	敎員	*giào yüen* geeow yeuehn
insubordination	違令	*wēi lìng* way ling
Intelligence Dept.	偵探部	*djen tàn bu* jun tan boo
interpreter	繙譯	*fan ih* fan ee
interval	間隔	*gièn gèh* gee'en geh
intrench, to	掘壕溝	*güeh hao gou* jeueh how gou
killed in action	陣亡	*djèn wāng* jun wang
knapsack	背囊	*bèi nāng* bay nang
ladder	梯子	*ti-dz* tee dz
rope ladder	繩梯	*shēng ti* shung tee
lance, spear	刺鎗	*tsī chiang* tsz cheeang

English	Chinese	Romanized Pronunciation
Lancer	長槍手	*chāng chiang shóu* chang cheeang shou
lashing (binding)	捆紮	*kwěn djàh* kwun ja
leave, on	告假	*gào gía* gow jeeah
left	左	*dzó* dzoh
— turn	向左	*hsìang dzó* sheeang dzo
— wheel	向左轉	*hsiàng dzó djwàn* sheeang dzo djwan
lieutenant (army)	千總	*chien dzúng* che'een dzung
— -colonel	參將	*tsan tsìang* tsan cheeang
— -general	副都統	*fù du túng* foo doo tung
line (rope)	繩子	*shēng-dz* shung dz
line, firing	排戰前行	*pāi djàn tsiēn hāng* pi jan chee'en hang
—, in	橫隊	*hwèn dùi* hwun dway
— of fire	射線	*shè hsìen* sheh shee'en
load, to (gun)	裝鎗	*djwang tsiang* djwang cheeang
magazine	火藥局	*hó yòh gǘh* ho yo jeu
— rifle	五響來福鎗	*wú hsiang lāi-fǘh tsiang* woo sheeang li foo cheeang
main body	大兵	*dà bing* dah bing
major	游擊	*yu gih* yeeoo gee
— -general	少將	*shao dziang* show jeeang
man-of-war	頭等兵艦	*tōu dĕng bing hsien* tou dung bing shee'en
map	地圖	*dì tū* dee too

English	Chinese	Romanized Pronunciation
March! (on the)	行軍	*hsing gün* shing jeun
—, forced	勉強行	*miên chiang hsing* mee'en cheeang shing
mark time, to	踏步	*dah bù* da boo
marksman	鎗準精兵	*tsiang djwên dzing bing* cheeang jwun dzing bing
midshipman	海軍學生	*hǎi gün hsioh seng* hi jeun sheeoh sung
military police	軍中巡警	*gün djung hsün ging* jeun jung sheun ging
mine	水雷	*shúi lūi* shway lway
minister of war	陸軍總長	*luh gün dzung djang* loo jeun dzung jeeang
musketry	鎗法	*tsiang fàh* cheeang fa
— instruction	敎練鎗法	*giào lìen tsiang fàh* geeow lee'en cheeang fa
muzzle of a gun	礮門	*pào mēn* pow mun
Navy, the	海軍	*hai gün* hi jeun
officer	武官	*wú gwan* woo gwan
—, non-com.	無印官	*wū yìn gwan* woo yin gwan
—, petty [(N.C.O.)	小官	*hsiǎo gwan* sheeow gwan
—, staff	參謀	*tsan mōu* tsan mou
officers' mess	官餐	*gwan tsan* gwan tsan
order (command)	號令	*hào lìng* how ling
orderly	傳令官	*chwān lìng gwan* chwan ling gwan
outpost	外哨	*wà. shao* wi show(ow as in now)
parade	排操	*pai tsao* pai tsow
parole	誓言	*shī yēn* shirr yen

English	Chinese	Romanized Pronunciation
Patrol	巡哨	*hsün shào* sheun show (ow as in now)
pay (officer's)	祿俸	*lùh fèng* loo fung
— (soldier's)	祿餉	*lùh hsiáng* loo sheeang
paymaster	發餉官	*fàh hsiang gwan* fa sheeang gwan
pickaxe	鶴嘴斧	*hoh dzúi fú* ho dzway foo
picket	一哨兵	*ih shào bing* ee show bing
pile arms!	架鎗	*già tsiang* jeeah cheeang
pontoon	浮橋	*fū chiao* foo cheeow
post	哨地	*shào di* show dee
present!	托鎗	*toh tsiang* toh cheeang
— arms!	舉鎗	*gü tsiang* geu cheeang
prisoner of war	俘囚	*fu tsiu* foo cheeoo
—, to take	捉人	*djoh rēn* jo run
promotion	提拔	*tī-bàh* tee ba
punishment	刑罰	*hsīng-fāh* shing fa
private, a	兵丁	*bing ding* bing ding
quartermaster	軍需官	*gün hsü gwan* jeun sheu gwan
— -sergeant	總軍需官	*dzùng gün shü gwan* Dzung jeun sheu gwan
quarters	寓所	*yü so* yeu soh
quick march!	快走	*kwài dzòu* kwi dzou
range of gun	礮程	*pào chēng* pow chung

English	Chinese	*Romanized* Pronunciation
Rank (in army)	官銜	*gwan hsien* gwan shee'en
— and file	兵士	*bing szï* bing siz
—, front	前隊	*chīen dùi* chee'en dway
—, rear	後隊	*hòu dùi* hou dway
rations	軍糧	*gün liáng* jeun leeang
ready!	預備	*yü bèi* yeu bay
rear, the	後哨	*hòu shào* hou show
rear-admiral	海軍少將	*hái gün shào dziang* hī jeun show jeeang
reconnaissance	考察地勢	*káo chàh dì shì* kow cha dee shirr
reconnoitre, to	窺探	*kwei tàn* kway tan
recruit, a	新兵	*hsin bing* shin bing
Red Cross Society	紅十字會	*hūng shïh dzì hwèi* hung shirr dz hway
redoubt	礮臺	*pào-tāi* pow tī
regiment, cavalry	聯隊馬軍	*lien dúi má gün* lee'en dway mah jeun
—, infantry	聯隊步兵	*liēn dùi bù bing* lee'en dway boo bing
regulations	軍法	*gün fàh* jeun fa
reins	馬韁	*má giang* mah jeeang
report, a	報告	*bào gào* bow gow
reserves	接應兵	*dzieh yìng bing* jee'eh ying bing
retire, retreat (to)	退後	*tùi hòu* tway hou
reveille	起號	*chì hào* chee how

English	Chinese	*Romanized* Pronunciation
Review	閱操	*yüèh tsao* yeueh tsow
rifle	來福鎗	*lai-fùh tsiang* li foo cheeang
right, the	右	*yù* yeeoo
— turn!	向右	*hsiàng yù* sheeang yeeoo
— wheel!	向右轉	*hsiàng yù djwǎn* sheeang yeeoo jwan
roll-call, the	點名	*dien ming* dee'en ming
route-march	行軍	*hsing gün* shing jeun
saddle	馬鞍	*má an* mah an
sailor, bluejacket	水師	*shúi szï* shway siz
— (merc. marine)	水手	*shúi shóu* shway shou
salute, a	軍禮	*gün lí* jeun lee
—, to	行軍禮	*hsing gün lí* shing jeun lee
scout, a	偵探	*djen tàn* jun tan
—, to	作偵探	*dzoh djen tàn* dzoh jun tan
sentry	哨兵	*shào bing* show bing
sergeant	哨長	*shào djáng* show jang
— -major	把總	*ba dzung* bah dzung
servant, officers'	聽差	*ting chai* ting chi
service (duty)	軍務	*gün wù* jeun woo
—, special	專役	*djwan yih* jwan yee
shell	礮彈	*pào dàn* pow dan

English	Chinese	*Romanized* Pronunciation
Shell fire	礮彈發	*bào-dàn fah* bow dan fa
shot, a	礮彈	*pào-dàn* pow dan
shoulder arms!	掮鎗	*gīen tsiang* jee'en cheeang
sight (of gun)	鎗準機	*tsiang djwĕn gi* cheeang jwun gee
signal, to	指揮	*djī hwei* jirr hway
signaller	指揮員	*djī hwei yüēn* jirr hway yeuehn
skirmish, to	小戰	*hsiáo djan* sheeow jan
skirmishers	小戰的人	*hsiao djan dy rēn* sheeow jan dee run
skirmishing	小戰的事	*hsiáo djan dy szī* sheeow jan dee siz
soldier	兵丁	*bing ding* bing ding
spade	鍬	*tsiao* cheeow
spy	探子	*tàn-dz* tan dz
squadron (cavalry)	騎兵隊	*chi bing dùi* chee bing dway
square	方陣	*fang djen* fang jun
staff, the	參謀官	*tsan mōu gwan* tsan mou gwan
stand at ease!	稍息	*sháo hsih* show shee
step, pace	步	*bù* boo
stirrup	踏蹬	*tàh deng* ta dung
store, ordnance-	軍火棧	*gün hó djan* jeun hoh jan
strategy	戰計	*djàn gi* jan gee
stretcher	檯床	*tāi chwāng* tie chwang

English	Chinese	*Romanized* Pronunciation
Stretcher-bearer	檯床夫	*tāi chwāng fu* ti chwang foo
supplies, field	押送戰物	*yàh sùng djàn wuh* ya sung djan wuh
supply column	接應兵	*dzieh yìng bing* jee'eh ying bing
surgeon	外科醫生	*wài ko i-seng* wi ko ee-sung
surround, to	圍困	*wēi kwèn* way kwun
sword	掛刀	*gwà dao* gwah dow
swords! carry	舉刀	*gü dao* geu dow
tactics	戰法	*djàn fàh* jan fa
tent	帳篷	*djang-pēng* jang pung
tent-peg	帳篷樁	*djàng-pēng djwang* jang pung jwang
torpedo	魚雷	*yü-lui* yeu lway
torpedo-boat	魚雷艇	*yü-lui tíng* yeu lway ting
— — destroyer	水雷驅擊艇	*shùi-lui chü gìh tíng* shway lway cheu gee ting
trenches	掘溝	*güēh gou* geueh gou
troops	兵	*bing* bing
unfix bayonets!	拔去刺刀	*bàh chù tsì dao* ba cheu tsz dow
uniform	號衣	*hào i* how ee
unlimber!	卸礮車	*hsìe pào che* sheeay pow cheh
veterinary surgeon	獸醫	*shòu-i* shou ee
volley	放一次鎗	*fàng ih tsï tsiang* fang ee tsz cheeang
volunteer, a	義兵	*ì bing* ee bing

English	Chinese	*Romanized* Pronunciation
wagon, a	軍車	*gün che* jeun cheh
war	打戰事	*dá djan szi* dah jan siz
water-bottle	水缾	*shúi piñg* shway ping
wheel, to	旋轉	*hsüen djwàn* sheuehn jwan
who goes there?	何人	*hō rĭn* ho run
works, earth-	泥礮臺	*ni pào-tai* nee pow ti
wound, a	傷口	*shang-kóu* shang kou
wounded, the	受傷者	*shòu shang djĕ* shou shang jeh

CONVERSATIONAL PHRASES AND SENTENCES

NOTE.—The Chinese equivalents are not in all cases literal translations, but are those which the same set of circumstances would draw from Chinese speakers.

Useful and Necessary Idiomatic Expressions and Phrases

談論話句

有益需用語合講法

English	Chinese	*Romanized* Pronunciation
Good morning!	早,早安	*dzáo; dzáo an* dzow; dzow an
good day; *or*, how do you do?	平安麼,你好麼	*pīng an mo? ní háo mo?* ping an mo? nee how mo?
good evening! (meeting)	晚見,晚安	*wán gièn; wán an* wan gee'en; wan an
good night! (to one going to bed)	再會,夜安	*dzài hwèi; yè an* dzi hway; yeh an
excuse me; *or*, I beg your pardon	對不住,原諒我	*dùi bùh dju; yüen liàng ó* dway boo joo; yeuehn lee-ang oh
oh, don't mention it!	呵,不要緊	*àh, bùh yào gín* ah, boo yow gin
thank you	謝謝你	*hsìe hsìe ní* sheeay sheeay nee
no, thank you	不阿,難爲你	*bùh àh, nān wèi ní* boo ah, nan way nee
thank you very much for your assistance	多謝你的幫助	*do hsìe nì dy bang dzu* doh sheeay nee dee bang-dzoo
thanks for your trouble	勞神勞神	*lāo shēn lāo shēn* low shun low shun

English	Chinese	*Romanized* Pronunciation
I apologise for interrupting you	攔閣下金言容我說一句	*lan gōh hsia gin yēn, yūng ó shwoh ih gü* lan goh sheeah gin yen, yung oh shwoh ee geu
it does not matter	不礙事	*bùh ài szì* boo **i** siz
I can scarcely ask (asking a favour)	我難以開口	*ó nān ì kai kóu* oh nan ee k**i** kou
please do, I beg	請便,請便	*chíng bièn, chíng bìen* ching bee'en, ching bee'en
you are a welcome guest	希客來了	*hsi kèh lāi liáo* shee keh l**i** leeow
just as you please	請你隨便	*ching ní sūi bièn* ching nee sway bee'en
you are quite right	你十分是	*ní shīh fen shì* nee shirr fun shirr
do as you please	隨你的便	*sūi ní dy bièn* sway nee dee bee'en
take as much as you please	多少隨你要	*do sháo sūi ní yào* doh show sway nee yow
it is lucky that...	幸虧	*hsìn kwēi* shin kway
as you, sir, know...	你先生曉得	*ní hsien seng hsiao dèh* nee shee'en sung sheeow deh
it must be done	必要作	*bìh yào dzoh* bee yow dzo
what are you doing? (*to* inferior)	你作甚麼	*ní dzòh shèn-mo?* nee dzo shun mo?
—(*to* equal *or* sup.)	先生作甚麼	*hsien seng dzòh shèn-mo* shee'en sung dzo shun mo?
please come back soon	請常過來	*chíng chāng kò lāi* ching chang ko l**i**
come here	這裏來	*dje lì lāi* jay lee l**i**
I have come on business	我有事情來	*ò yú szì tsīng lāi* oh yeeoo siz ching l**i**
when will you come?	你幾時要來	*ní gi shī yào lāi?* nee gee shirr yow l**i**?
will you come?	你肯來麼	*ní kěn lāi, mo?* nee kun l**i** mo?
where are you going?	你那裏去	*ní ná lì chü?* nee nah lee cheu?

English	Chinese	Romanized Pronunciation
Go and look	去看看	*chü kàn kàn* cheu kan kan
what is the matter?	甚麼事	*shen mo szï?* shun mo siz?
or, what is it?	or 甚麼東西	*shen mo dung hsi?* shun mo dung sheer
as soon as possible	趕快	*gán kwài* gan kwi
oh no! that is not so	呵不,那不是這樣	*àh buh; nà bùh shï djè yàng* ah boo; nah boo shirr jeh yang
if possible	倘若可以	*táng ròh kó i* tang ro ko ee
I don't quite understand	我不十分懂	*ó bùh shïh fen dúng* oh boo shirr fun dung
I haven't the slightest idea	我一點不曉得	*ó ih dién bùh hsiáo deh* oh ee dee'en boo sheeow deh
what does this mean?	這是甚麼意思	*djè shì shèn-mo ì-szï?* jeh shirr shun mo ee siz?
I don't know	我不曉得	*ó búh hsiao dèh* oh boo sheeow deh
I have never seen it	我沒有見過	*ó mūh yú gìen gò* oh moo yeeoo gee'en go
I haven't seen you for a long time	久違久違	*gíu wēi gíu wēi* geeoo way geeoo way
what do you say?	你怎樣講	*ní dzén yàng giang?* nee dzun yang geeang?
who said so?	那一個說的	*ná ïh go shwoh dy?* nah ee go shwo dee?
I will speak to him about it	我同他說這話	*ó tūng ta shwoh djè hùa* oh tung tah shwo jeh hwah
he won't hear of it	他不肯聽	*ta bùh kén tīng* tah boo kun ting
he cannot be relied on	他靠不住	*ta kào bùh dju* tah kow boo joo
he is honest and hard-working	他是老實肯做	*ta shï láo-shïh kén dz* tah shirr low shirr kun dzoh

English	Chinese	*Romanized* Pronunciation
You must not do that	這個事你做不得	*dje go szĭ nĭ dzo bùh dĕh* jeh go siz nee dzoh boo deh
don't tell anyone	不要告訴人	*bùh yào gào sù rĕn* boo yow gow soo run
I will do my best	我儘力做	*ŏ dzìn lìh dzo* oh dzin lee dzoh
I can do without it	我沒有也不要緊	*ŏ mūh yú yĕ bùh yào gín* oh moo yeeoo yeh boo yow gin
it will do afterwards	後來也可以	*hòu lāi yĕ kŏ ĭ* hou li yeh ko ee
it will do at your leisure	你得空可以	*nĭ dĕh kùng kŏ ĭ* nee deh kung ko ee
be careful!	當心	*dang hsin* dang shin
I will bring it for you	我替你帶來	*ŏ tì nĭ dài lāi* oh tee nee di li
do you want this?	你要這個不要	*nĭ yào dje gò bùh yào?* nee yow jeh go boo yow?
I want an answer	我要回信	*o yào hwēi hsìn* oh yow hway shin
wait a moment	等一刻	*dĕng ih kĕh* dung ee keh
what is your answer?	你怎樣答應	*nĭ dzĕn yàng dàh yìng?* nee dzun yang da ying?
do you like this?	你喜歡這個麼	*nĭ hsĭ hwan djè gò mo?* nee shee hwan jeh go moh?
I like it very much	我很喜歡	*ŏ hĕn hsĭ hwan* oh hun shee hwan
how do you like it?	你喜歡怎樣的	*nĭ hsĭ hwan dzen yàng dy?* nee shee hwan dzun yang dee?
kindly let me know at once	請卽刻告訴我	*chĭng dzih kĕh gào sù ŏ* ching jee keh gow soo oh
you are very fortunate	你運氣好	*nĭ yün chì hăo* nee yeuin chee how

English	Chinese	Romanized Pronunciation
You need not be anxious	不必罣念	*bùh bìh gwa nien* boo bee gwah lee'en
it is too difficult	這個事太難	*dje gò szï tài nán* jeh go siz tī nan
it is well done	作的很好	*dzoh dy hĕn hào* dzo dee hun how
what is your address?	你住在那裏	*nì djù dzài ná-lì* nee joo dzī nah lee
my address is...	我住在...	*ó djù dzài...* oh joo dzī...
this is my address	這是我的住址	*dje shï ó dy djù djï* jeh shirr oh dee joo jirr
give me his address	請你告訴我他的住址	*chǐng nì gao su ó ta dy dju djï* ching nee gow soo oh tah dee joo jirr
he lives in Pekin	他住在北京	*ta djù dzài Bĕh-ging* tah joo dzī Pekin
he resides at Nankin	他在南京住	*ta dzài Nān-ging djù* tah dzī Nankin joo
so it seems. (yes, I suppose so)	我想是不錯	*ó hsiáng shï bùh tso* o sheeang shirr boo tsoh
do you speak English?	你會說英話麽	*nì hwèi shwoh Ying-gwoh hwà mo* nee hway shwo Ying gwo hwah moh
I am English	我是英國人	*ó shï Ying-gwoh rĕn* o shirr Ying gwo run
I don't understand	我不懂	*ó bùh dúng* o boo dung
I can speak a little Chinese	我會說幾句中國話	*ó hwèi shwoh gì gü Djung-gwoh hwa* o hway shwo gee geu Jung gwoh hwah
I had not time	我沒有工夫	*ó mŭh yú gung fu* o moo yoo gung foo
I really cannot wait	我實在不能等	*ó shïh dzài bùh nĕng dĕng* o shirr dzī boo nung dung
as you see	你看看	*nì kàn kàn* nee kan kan

English	Chinese	*Romanized* Pronunciation
Where were you seen?	他在那裏看見你	*ta dzài ná lì kàn gien ni* tah dzi nah lee kan gee'en nee
is it convenient to-morrow?	明天得便不得便	*mīng tien deh bìen buh deh bìen* ming tee'en deh bee'en boo deh bee'en
I will return it to-morrow	我明天送回來	*ó mīng tien sùng hwēi lāi* o ming tee'en sung hway li
just as you like	隨你的便	*sūi ní dy bìen* sway nee dee bee'en
please let me know immediately	請你卽刻寫信給我	*chíng ní dzih kèh hsie hsin gih ó* ching nee jee keh sheeay shin gee o
he has already left	他已經走了	*ta ì ging dzóu liao* tah ee ging dzou leeow
he probably does not know	光景他不知道	*gwang ging ta bùh djī dào* gwang ging tah boo jirr dow
this article wears well	這個東西耐久	*dje gò dung hsi nài gíu* jeh go dung shee ni geeoo
are there any book-shops in Shanghai	上海有書坊麼	*Shànghái yú shu fang mo?* Shanghai yeeoo shoo fang mo?
to be sure there are!	那自然,書坊多咯	*nà dzī ran; shu fang do lòh* na diz ran; shoo fang doh lo
I enquired, but there was none	我問過了,那裏沒有	*ó wèn gò liáo; na lì mūh yu* o wun go leeow; na lee moo yeeoo
I see you for the first time	我們是初次見面	*ó mēn shī tsu tzī gìen mìen* o mun shirr tsoo tsz gee'en mee'en
where are you going?	你到那裏去	*ní dào ná-lì chū* nee dow nah lee cheu
come here; I have something for you to do	你來,這裏有事	*ní lāi; dje lì yú szī* nee li; jeh lee yeeoo siz
may I ask who you are, sir?	請問先生,你是那一個	*chíng wēn hsien seng ní shī na ih go* ching wun shee'en sung nee shirr nah ee go

English	Chinese	*Romanized* Pronunciation
When do you return to Europe?	你幾時回歐洲	*ni gi shï hwēi Ou-djou?* nee gee shirr hway Ou-jou?
is anything the matter with you?	甚麼事叫你不暢快	*shèn mo szï giao ni bùh shwang kwài?* shun moh siz geeow nee boo shwang kwi?
who said so?	是那個說的	*shï ná gò shwoh dy?* shirr nah go shwo dee?
be pleased to wait	請等一等	*chíng déng ih déng* ching dung ee dung
go and wait at the school, please	你可以到學堂裏去等	*ni kó i dào hsioh tāng li chü déng* nee ko ee dow sheeoh tang lee cheu dung
you come as well	你也來罷	*ni yé lāi bà* nee yeh li bah
I am told he returned yesterday	聽說他昨天回來的	*ting shwoh ta dzoh tien hwēi lāi dy* ting shwo tah dzo tee'en hway li dee
you must be careful	你要小心	*ni yào hsiao hsin* nee yow sheeow shin
I did not break it; *i.e.*, it was not I who broke it	不是我打破的	*bùh shï ó dá pò dy* boo shirr o dah po dee
that is the important point	這是頂要緊的	*dje shï ding yào gin dy* jeh shirr ding yow gin dee
why?	爲甚麼	*wèi shen mo?* way shun moh?
in that case it is all right	這樣就是不錯	*dje yàng dziu shï bùh tso* jeh yang jeeoo shirr boo tsoh
it is extremely inconvenient	這是很不便當	*dje shï hén buh bien dang* jeh shirr hun boo bee'en dang
there is no help for it	沒有法子	*mūh yú fàh-dzï* moo yeeoo fa dz
under what circumstances?	有甚麼情形	*yú shen mo tsīng hsīng?* yeeoo shun mo ching shing?
what is the reason?	甚麼緣故	*shen mo yüen gù?* shun mo yeuehn goo?

English	Chinese	*Romanized* Pronunciation
What is the matter?	有甚麼事情	*yú shèn mo szï tsïng?* yeeoo shun mo siz ching?
there is no mistake about it!	一點不錯	*ïh diĕn bùh tso* ee dee'en boo tso
you were certainly to blame	一定你有錯處	*ïh dìng nĭ yú tso chù* ee ding nee yeeoo tso choo
what is your opinion?	你的意見如何	*nĭ dy ì gìen rū hŏ?* nee dee ee gee'en roo ho?
please make a note of it	請你記下來	*tsíng nĭ gì hsìa lāi* ching nee gee sheeah li
I say! Mr....	先生請來	*hsien seng tsĭng lāi* shee'en sung ching li
look!	你看	*nĭ kàn!* nee kan!
it is indeed grand	實在好看	*shïh dzai hǎo kàn* shirr dzi how kan
without ceremony	不拘禮	*bùh gü lĭ* boo geu lee
speak louder, please	請說高一點	*tsíng shwoh gao ïh diĕn* ching shwo gow ee dee'en
is it not beautiful?	不是頂好看嗎	*bùh shï ding hǎo kàn ma* boo shirr ding how kan mah

Expressions of Emotion

動 情 詞

English	Chinese	*Romanized* Pronunciation
Indeed! (is that so?)	眞是這樣的麼	*djen shï dje yàng dy mo?* jun shirr jeh yang dee mo?
how can you say such a thing!	這個話你怎麼能說呢	*dje gó hwa nĭ dzĕn mo nĕng shwoh nĭ?* jeh go hwah nee dzun mo nung shwo nee?

English	Chinese	Romanized Pronunciation
It is a pity that...	很可惜	*hěn kǒ hsih* hun ko shee
I am sorry for you	我看你可憐	*ǒ kàn nǐ kǒ lien* o kan nee ko lee'en
I see!	是啊,我懂了	*shī o! ǒ dúng liáo* shirr oh! o dung leeow
excuse me for having inconvenienced you†	難爲你,請不要見怪	*nān wèi nǐ* (or) *tsǐng bùh yào gièn gwài* nan way nee (or) ching boo yow gee'en gwi
what! (protest)	甚麼話	*shèn mo hwà!* shun mo hwah?
what a pity!	可惜	*kǒ hsih!* ko shee!
I feel ashamed	我慚愧	*ǒ tsan gwei* o tsan gway
it is a nuisance	實在可惡	*shǐh dzai kǒ wù* shirr dzi ko woo
it *was* jolly!	眞正暢快	*djen djèng chāng kwài* jun jung chang kwi
I am very glad of it	那我就很歡喜	*nà ǒ dziu hěn hwan hsǐ* nah o jeeoo hun hwan shee
I ām delighted	我歡喜得很	*ǒ hwan hsǐ dèh hěn* o hwan shee deh hun
I am glad	我很快活	*ǒ hěn kwai hòh* o hun kwi ho
I congratulate you	恭喜你	*gung hsǐ nǐ* gung shee nee
don't talk nonsense!	不要胡說	*bùh yào hú shwoh* boo yow hoo shwo
don't make such a noise!	不要鬧事	*bùh yào nào szï* boo yow now siz
don't bother!	不要多事	*bùh yào do szï* boo yow doh siz
it is most annoying!	這個事慪人	*dje gò szï òu rēn* jeh go siz ou run
I don't care!	我不管	*ǒ bùh gwǎn* o boo gwan
this won't do!	這個不行	*dje go bùh hsīng* jeh go boo shing

English	Chinese	*Romanized* Pronunciation
I should never think of saying such a thing!	這個話我萬不能說	*dje gò hwà ó wàn bùh nĕng shwoh* jeh go hwah o wan boo nung shwo
—of doing such a thing!	這個事萬不能作	*dje gò szï wàn bùh nĕng dzoh* jeh go siz wan boo nung dzo
it is none of your business	不與你相干	*bùh yü ní hsiang gan* boo yeu nee sheeang gan
you had better hold your tongue	你不要提那個話	*ní bùh yào tī nà gò hwà* nee boo yow tee nah go hwa
do as I order you!	你照我講的作	*ní djao ó giáng dy dzoh* nee jow o geeang dee dzo
you have my strict orders	我已經仔細的吩咐你	*ó í ging dzi hsi dy fen-fù ní* o ee ging dz shee dee fun foo nee
why don't you go when I tell you?	我叫你你何以不去	*ó giao ní ní hō í bùh chü?* o geeow nee nee ho ee boo cheu?
get away, *or* be off!	你去罷	*ní chü bà* nee cheu bah
get out of the way and let me pass!	站過去讓我走	*djan gò chü, ràng ó dzóu* jan go cheu, rang o dzou
insolent fellow!	你這個人混賬	*ní dje gò rén hwèn djang* nee jeh go run hwun jang

MARLBOROUGH'S *SELF-TAUGHT* SERIES includes the following *Oriental* Languages:—

HINDUSTANI	PERSIAN	ARABIC (Syrian)
JAPANESE	SINHALESE	EGYPTIAN (Arabic)
BURMESE	TAMIL	

Also all the principal *European* languages, and LATIN. The Series is constantly being extended.

A catalogue will be sent free on application to the Publishers.

Enquiries

NOTE.—In asking for information, it is usual to preface any enquiry with the formula "*Ching wên !*" (Inform me please), whether the query be addressed to a male or a female. The formula used in thanking a stranger for information received is "*sheeay sheeay nee !*"—the English equivalent of which is "Thanks very much."

English	Chinese	*Romanized* Pronunciation
What is the Chinese name for this?	中國話這個叫甚麼東西	*Djung gwoh hwà djè gò gìao shen mo dung hsi?* Jung gwo hwah jeh go geeow shun mo dung shee?
what is this made of?	這是甚麼作的	*djè shï shèn mo dzoh dy?* jeh shirr shun mo dzo dee?
what is this thing?	這是甚麼東西	*djè shï shèn mo dung hsi?* jeh shirr shun mo dung shee?
what ought I to do?	我應該怎樣作	*ó ying gai dzen yàng dzoh?* o ying gbi dzun yang dzō?
what is this for?	這是甚麼用處	*djè shï shèn mo yung chù?* jeh shirr shun mo yung choo?
what is he doing?	他作甚麼事	*ta dzoh shèn mo szï?* tah dzō shun mo siz?
what have you come for?	你來甚麼事	*ní lāi shèn-mo szï?* nee li shun mo siz?
what could have been the reason?	到底甚麼緣故呢	*dào dí shèn mo yüen gù ni?* dow dee shun mo yeuehn goo nee?
what is it all about?	是甚麼事	*shï shèn mo szï?* shirr shun-mo siz?
what do you propose to do?	你用甚麼法子呢	*ní yùng shèn mo fàh-dz ni?* nee yung shun-mo fah dz nee?

English	Chinese	*Romanized* Pronunciation
What has happened to him?	他遇見甚麼事	*ta yü gièn shèn mo szï?* tah yeu gee'en shun mo siz?
what is your name?	請問貴姓	*chǐng-wèn, gwèi hsìng?* ching wun, gway shing?
my name is Lee	我姓李	*ó shìng lǐ* o shing lee
what time does the lecture begin to morrow?	明天幾點鐘演說	*mīng tien gǐ diěn djung yěn shwoh?* ming tee'en gee dee'en jung yen shwo?
you had better enquire	不如細細明問	*bùh rū hsì hsì mīng wèn* boo roo shee shee ming wun
please enquire for me (on my behalf)	請你替我問	*chǐng ní tì ó wèn* ching nee tee o wun
I will enquire for you	好，我替你問	*háo, ó tì ní wèn* how, o tee nee wun
what salary should I pay per month?	我當每月給他多少薪水	*ó dang měi yüeh gih ta do sháo hsin shúi?* o dang may yeueh gee tah doh show shin shway?
Oh! I should say... would be sufficient	依我看來……可以咯	*i ó kàn lāi...kǒ-i loh* ee o kan li...ko ee lo
what age are you?	尊庚多少	*dzwen geng do sháo?* dzun gung doh show?
which is the shortest way to...?	到……那一條路近些	*dào...ná īh tīao lù gin hsie?* dow...nah ee teeow loo gin sheeay?
is this the way to...?	到……走那一條路	*dào...dzóu ná īh tīao lù?* dow...dzou nah ee teeow loo?
how far is it to...?	到……有多遠	*dào...yú doh yüěn?* dow...yeeoo do yeuehn?
now far is it from here?	離這裏多遠	*lí djè lǐ do yüén?* lee jeh lee doh yeuehn?
where is the police station?	警察局在那裏	*gíng chǎh güh dzài ná lǐ* ging cha geu dzi nah lee

English	Chinese	*Romanized* Pronunciation
Does Mr....live in this street?	…先生住在這條街上麽	*...hsien-seng djù dzài djè lĭao giāi shàng mo?* ...shee'en-sung joo dzī jeh teeow gee'ī shang mo?
can you direct me to his house?	你可以指我他住在那裏	*ni kó i djī ó ta djù dzài ná lĭ* nee ko ee jirr o tah joo dzī nah lee
where does he live?...	他在那裏住	*ta dzài ná li djù?* tah dzī nah lee joo?
can I see Mr....?	…先生在家麽	*...hsien seng dzài gia mo?* ..shee'en sung dzī geeah mo?
having made enquiry	已經問過了	*i ging wèn kò liáo* ee ging wun go leeow
when do you return to your country?	你幾時回國去	*ni gi shī hwēi gwoh chü?* nee gee shirr hway gwo cheu?
isn't it finished yet?	還沒有作好麽	*hwān mūh yú dzoh háo mo?* hwan moo yeeoo dzo how mo?
is it convenient today?	今天便當麽	*gin tien bìen dang mo?* gin tee'en bee'en dang mo?

Travelling: By Railway

(For Vocabulary see pages 59-64.)

搭 火 車

English	Chinese	*Romanized* Pronunciation
Order a carriage to take me to the station	叫馬車送我到火車站	*giào má che sùng ó dào hò che djan* geeow mah cheh sung o dow ho cheh jan
to the station, quick!	到火車站,快點	*dào hò che djan, kwai dién* dow ho cheh jan, kwī dee'en
hurry up!	快些	*kwai hsie* kwī sheeay

English	Chinese	Romanized Pronunciation
Shall I be in time?	趕得上麼	*gán dèh shàng mo?* gan deh shang mo?
let us go	我們可以去	*ó mēn kó ì chü* o mun ko ee cheu
I think I shall go	我想要去	*o hsiáng yào chü* o sheeang yow cheu
the first train in the morning	早上第一車	*dzào shàng dī ih che* dzow shang dee ee chay
I shall set off to-morrow	我想明天去	*ó hsiáng mīng tien chü* o sheeang ming tee'en cheu
there is plenty of time	還早	*hwān dzáo* hwan dzow
is the luggage ready?	行李預備好了麼	*hsīng lì yü bèi háo liáo mo?* shing lee yeu bay how leeow mo?
please help me with my luggage	請你替我搬行李	*chíng ní tì ó ban hsīng lì* ching nee tee o ban shing lee
which is your luggage?	你的行李在那裏	*ní dy hsīng lì dzai ná lì* nee dee shing lee dzi nah lee
will you take charge of my luggage?	請你看著我的行李	*chíng ní kàn djoh ó dy hsīng lì* ching nee kan jo o dee shing lee
take care!	小心	*hsiáo sin* sheeow shin
are you sure you have forgotten nothing?	沒有忘記甚麼東西麼	*mūh-yú wāng gì shèn-mo dung hsi mo?* moo yeeoo wang gee shun mo dung shee mo?
I will go and get a ticket	我去買票	*ó chü mái pìao* o cheu mi peeow
where is the booking-office?	票房在那裏	*pìao fang dzai ná lì?* peeow fang dzi nah lee?
give me a first-class return to Chentu	給我上成都的頭等來回票	*gih ó shàng Chēntu dy tōu deng lāi hwei pìao* gee o shang Chentoo dee tou dung li hway peeow

English	Chinese	*Romanized* Pronunciation
I want return tickets	我要來回票	*ó yào lāi hwei pìao* o yow lī hway peeow
1st class; 2nd; 3rd	頭等二等三等	*tōu déng, èr déng, san déng* tou dung, ur dung, san dung
where are you going, sir?	先生到那裏去	*hsien-seng dào nà-lí chü?* shee'en sung dow nah lee [cheu?
I am going through to...	我要到…	*ó yào dào...* o yow dow...
all right, come along	不錯,往這裏來	*bùh tso, wáng dje lí lāi* boo tsoh, wang jeh lee lī
what is the fare?	車費多少	*che fèi do sháo?* cheh fay doh show?
how much is the excess? (on luggage)	行李多,每百磅重多少錢	*hsing lí do, méi bēh bàng djùng do sháo tsīen?* shing lee doh, may beh bang jung, doh show chee'en?
when is the next train for...?	下班車往……幾點鐘開	*hsìa ban che wáng......gī dìen jung kai?* sheeah ban cheh wang...... gee dee'en jung kī?
is this the train for...?	這可是往……的車子	*dje kó shì wáng...dy che-dz?* jeh ko shirr wang......dee cheh dz?
what time is there a train for...?	幾點鐘有車子往……	*gī dièn djung yú che-dz wáng......?* gee dee'en jung yeeoo cheh dz wang......?
when will the train start?	甚麼時候開車	*shèn mo shī hòu kai che?* shun mo shirr hou kī cheh?
at once, sir	馬上就開車	*má shàng dziu kai che* mah shang jeeoo kī cheh
is there a non-smoking carriage?	有不准吃煙的車子麼	*yú bùh djwen chīh yen dy che-dz mo?* yeeoo boo jwun chirr yen dee cheh dz mo?
where is your ticket, please?	請看票子	*chíng kàn pìao dz* ching kan peeow dz
is this an express?	這是快車麼	*dje shì kwai che mo?* jeh shirr kwī cheh mo?

English	Chinese	Romanized Pronunciation
Am I in the right train for...?	到……這個車子錯不錯	*dào......djè gò che-dz tso bùh tso?* dow......jeh go cheh dz tso boo tso?
where do I change for...?	到……要在那裏換車	*dào......yào dzài ná lǐ hwàn che?* dow......yow dzi nah lee hwan cheh?
there! the train is starting	看,車要開了	*kàn! che yào kai liáo* kan! cheh yow ki leeow
that seat is engaged	那個座已經定	*nà gò dzo ì gìng ding liào* nah go dzo ee ging ding leeow
do I change here for...?	到…當在這裏換車麼	*dào...dang dzài djè lǐ hwan che mo?* dow...dang dzi jeh lee hwan cheh mo?
this is not a smoking carriage	這是不准吃烟的車子	*djè shī bùh djwen chīh yen dy che-dz* jeh shirr boo jwun chirr yen dee cheh dz
do you object to smoking?	你不喜歡人吃煙麼	*ní bùh hsi hwan rēn chīh yen mo?* nee boo shee hwan run chirr yen mo?
may I open (close) the window?	我可以開(關)這個牕戶麼	*ó kó ǐ kai (gwan) djè gò chwang hù mo?* o ko ee ki (gwan) jeh go chwang hoo mo?
do we stop long here?	在這裏停車的工夫大不大	*dzài djè lí tīng che dy gung-fu dà bùh dà?* dzi jeh lee ting cheh dee gung foo dah boo dah?
show these ladies to the waiting room	你可以帶這些女客到女客房	*ní kó ǐ dài djè hsie nü kèh dào nü kèh fàng* nee ko ee di cheh sheeay neu keh dow neu keh fang
lavatory	便房	*bìen fāng* bee'en fang
which is the way out?	出去走那裏	*chuh chü dzou ná lǐ?* choo cheu dzou nah lee?
there is the way out	這是出路	*djè shī chuh lù* jeh shirr choo loo
I have come to meet you, sir	我來迎接先生	*ó lāi yìn dzìeh hsien-seng* o li yin jeeay shee'en-sung

By Road: Hiring Conveyances

(See Vocabulary pages 59-64.)

旱 路 雇 車

English	Chinese	*Romanized* Pronunciation
Order a 'riksha	喊東洋車	*hán dung yāng che* han dung yang cheh
here! jinriksha-man!	東洋車,來	*dung yāng che, lāi* dung yang cheh, li
here! bring two 'rikshas	喊兩部東洋車來	*hán liáng bù dung yāng che lāi* han leeang boo dung yang cheh li
a carriage with two horses	要雙馬車	*yào shwang má che* yow shwang mah cheh
here! bring one 'riksha	喊一部東洋車	*hán ih bù dung yāng che* han ee boo dung yang cheh
a 'riksha drawn by two men	兩個人拉的東洋車	*liáng gò rēn la dy dung yāng che* leeang go run lah dee dung yang cheh
a 'riksha to seat two persons	坐得下兩個人的東洋車	*dzo dèh hsià liáng gò rēn dy dung yāng che* dzo deh sheeah leeang go run dee dung yang cheh
how much to take me to Siccawei	送我到徐家匯要多少錢	*sùng ó dào Hsü gia wèi yào do shǎo tsiēn* sung o dow Sheu geeah way yow doh show chee'en
how many are there in your party?	你一陣有幾個人	*ní ih djèn yú gi gò rēn* nee ee jun yeeoo gee go run
there are four of us	我們一陣四個人	*ó mēn ih djèn szì gò rēn* o mun ee jun siz go run
take me to the station	送我到火車站	*sùng ó dào hó che djan* sung o dow ho cheh jan
all right, please step in	請你上車	*tsing ní shàng che* ching nee shang cheh

English	Chinese	Romanized Pronunciation
Will he be able to go?	到…他能去嗎	*dào……ta nĕng chü ma?* dow……ta nung cheu ma?
put up the nood	車篷拉起來	*che pēng la chi lai* cheh pung lah chee li
lower the hood	車篷放下去	*che pēng fàng hsia chü* cheh pung fang sheeah cheu
stop here a moment	車子停一刻	*che-dz ting ih kĕh* cheh dz ting ee keh
let me get out here	我要下來	*ó yào hsia lai* o yow sheeah li
how far is it to…?	到……多少路	*dào……do sháo lù* dow……doh show loo
which is the road to:..?	到……走那一條路	*dào…dzóu ná ih tiao lù* dow…dzou nah ee teeow loo
how is the road ahead?	前面的路好走不好走	*chien mien dy lù háo dzóu bùh háo dzóu* chee'en mee'en dee loo how dzou boo how dzou
please tell me the way to Jessfield	請問到王家渡走那一條路	*ching wèn dào Wāng gia dù dzóu ná ih tiao lù* ching wen dow Wang geeah doo dzou nah ee teeow loo
will it be possible to go?	能走得到麼	*nĕng dzóu dĕh dào mo?* nung dzou deh dow mo?
your horse is ready, sir	先生你的馬巳預備好了	*hsien seng ní dy má i yü-bèi háo liáo* shee'en sung nee dee mah ee yeu bay how leeow
it is no distance on to the next place	到下站沒有多遠	*dào hsia djàn mūh-yú do yüén* dow sheeah jan moo yeeoo doh yeuehn
how many lee is it from here?	離這裏多少里	*lì djè lí do sháo lí* lee jeh lee doh show lee
how dreadfully bad the road is!	這個路實在壞的很	*djè gò lù shĭh dzài hwài dy hĕn* jeh go loo shirr dzi hwi dee hun

English	Chinese	*Romanized* Pronunciation
How many lee is it to the next town?	到前面的碼頭有幾里路	*dào chiēn mìen dy mà tōu yú gí lí lù?* dow chee'en mee'en dee mah tou yeeoo gee lee loo
must I go straight on?	可是筆直走麼	*kó shī bĭh djĭh dzóu mo?* ko shirr bee jirr dzou mo?

By Steamboat

(For Vocabulary see pages 64-65.)

火 輪 船

English	Chinese	*Romanized* Pronunciation
When do we start?	我們幾時動身	*ó mēn gí shī dùng shen?* o mun jee shirr dung shun?
send the steward to me	喊侍者來	*hán shī dje lāi* han shirr jeh li
what is the first-cabin fare?	坐大艙多少錢	*dzo dà tsang do sháo tsiēn?* dzo dah tsang doh show chee'en?
please show me my state-room	我的房間在那裏	*ó dy fāng gièn dzài ná-lí?* o dee fang gee'en dzi nah lee?
is this berth taken?	這個鋪位有人定了沒有	*djè gò pù wèi yú rēn dìng liáo muh-yú?* jeh go poo way yeeoo run ding leeow moo yeeoo?
where is the captain?	船主在那裏	*chwān djú dzài ná lí* chwan joo dzi nah lee?
I will engage the whole cabin	這全間我都定了	*djè chüen gièn ó du tìng liáo* jeh cheuehn gee'en o doo ding leeow
put my bag in the cabin	拏我的皮包送到房間裏去	*nā ó dy pī bao sùng dào fāng gièn lí chü* nah o dee pee bow sung dow fang gee'en lee cheu

English	Chinese	Romanized Pronunciation
Have you a passport?	你有護照沒有	*ní yú hù djao muh yú?* nee yeeoo hoo jow moo yeeoo?
what is the number of your cabin?	你的房間是那一號	*nì dy fāng gièn shì nǎ ih hào?* nee dee fang gee'en shirr nah ee how?
I am in number three	我是第三號	*ó shì dì san hào* o shirr dee san how
will it be smooth?	海水平靜麼	*hái shúi pīng dzìng mo?* hi shway ping jing mo?
the sea is rough	海裏浪很大	*hái lì làng hén dà* hai lee lang hun dah
is she a good boat?	是一個好船麼	*shì ih gò háo chwān mo?* shirr ee go how chwan mo?
shall you stay on deck?	你要在艙面坐坐麼	*ni yào dzài tsang mièn dzo dzo mo?* nee yow dzi tsang mee'en dzo dzo mo?
no, I shall go below	不,我要下去	*bùh, ó yào hsìa chü* boo, o yow sheeah cheu
I feel very sick	暈船的很	*yün chwān dèh hén* yeuin chwan deh hun
I am going below to my cabin	我要下到房間去	*ó yào hsìa dào fāng gièn chü* o yow sheeah dow fang-gee'en cheu
can we have dinner on board?	我們可以在船上吃中飯麼	*ó mēn kó ì dzài chwān shàng chīh djung fàn mo?* o mun ko ee dzi chwan shang chirr jung fan mo?
open (shut) the port-hole	開(關)牕戶	*kai (gwan) chwang hù* ki (gwan) chwang hoo
here! sanpan!	舢板來	*sanbàn lāi!* sanpan li!
how much to take me ashore?	送我上坡幾個錢	*sùng ó shàng po gí gò tsien* sung o shang po gee go chee'en
please let me see your passport	請你給我護照看	*ching ní kih ó hù djao kàn* ching nee gee o hoo jow kan

Arrival

(See Vocabulary pages 59-64.)

到 了 碼 頭

English	Chinese	Romanized Pronunciation
Here is my luggage	我的行李在這裏	*ó dy hsīng lí dzài djè lí* o dee shing lee dzi jeh lee
where is the custom-house?	稅關在那裏	*shùi gwan dzai ná lí?* shway gwan dzi nah lee?
bring that trunk to the custom-house	拏那個箱子送到稅關去	*nā nà gò hsiang-dzī sùng dào shùi gwan chü* nah nah go sheeang-dz sung dow shway gwan cheu
have you anything to declare?	箱子裏有當完稅的東西麼	*hsiang-dzī li yú dang wān shùi dy dung hsi mo?* sheeang-dz lee yeeoo dang wan shway dee dung shee mo?
I have nothing dutiable	沒有報稅的東西	*mūh yú bào shùi dy dung hsi* moo yeeoo bow shway dee dung shee
please give me your keys	請你拏鑰匙給我	*tsing ní nā yōh chī gíh ó* ching nee nah yo chirr gee o
here are the keys	鑰匙在這裏	*yōh chī dzai dje lí* yo chirr dzi jeh lee
is there an omnibus?	有公共馬車麼	*yú gung gùng má che mo?* yeeoo gung gung mah cheh mo?
call a carriage	喊馬車	*hán má che* han mah cheh
there is no carriage	沒有馬車	*mūh yú má che* moo yeeoo ma cheh
what is the fare to the hotel?	坐馬車到客寓多少錢	*dzo má che dào kèh yü do sháo tsīen?* dzo mah cheh dow keh yeu doh show chee'en?
tell the driver where to take me	你告訴馬夫送我到那裏	*ní gào sù má fu sùng ó dào nà lí* nee gow soo mah foo sung o dow nah-lee

The Hotel

(See Vocabulary pages 37-41.)

到客寓

English	Chinese	*Romanized* Pronunciation
Is the proprietor anywhere about?	主人在家麼	*djú rēn dzài gia mo?* joo run dzi geeah mo?
have you a room vacant?	有空房間麼	*yú kung fāng gien mo?* yeeoo kung fang gee'en mo?
I want two or three rooms	我要兩三個房間	*ó yào liáng san gò fāng gièn* o yow leeang san go fang gee'en
have you a larger room?	有比這個大的房間麼	*yú bí dje gò dà dy fāng gièn mo?* yeeoo bee jeh go dah dee fang gee'en mo?
this room is too small	這個房間太小	*dje gò fāng gièn tai hsiáo* jeh go fang gee'en ti sheeow
show me a bed-room	你給我看睡覺的房子	*ní gíh ó kàn shùi giao dy fāng-dzï* nee gee o kan shway geeow dee fang-dz
I will take this one	我就定這個房間	*ó dzìu dìng dje gò fāng gièn* o jeeoo ding jeh go fang gee'en
have you no better ones?	你沒有比這個好些的麼	*ní mūh yú bí dje gò háo hsie dy mo?* nee moo yeeoo bee jeh go how sheeay dee mo?
have you not a cooler room?	你沒有涼快的房間麼	*nì mūh yú liáng kwài dy fāng gièn mo?* nee moo yeeoo leeang kwi dee fang gee'en mo?
I want a large one	我要一個大房間	*ó yào ih gò dà fāng gièn* o yow ee go dah fang gee'en

English	Chinese	*Romanized* Pronunciation
Show me some nice rooms	你給我看些上等的房間	*ní gĭh ó kàn hsíe shàng dĕng dy fāng gièn* nee gee o kan sheeay shang dung dee fang gee'en
how much do you charge per day?	要多少錢一天	*yao do sháo tsĭen ĭh tien?* yow doh show chee'en ee tee'en?
has my luggage come?	我的行李來了麼	*ó dy hsīng lĭ lāi liáo mo?* o dee shing lee li leeow mo?
send the luggage upstairs	拏行李送到樓上	*nā hsīng lí sùng dào lōu shàng* na shing lee sung dow lou shang
put it down here	放在這裏	*fàng dzài djè lĭ* fang dzi jeh lee
do you intend to stay long?	你要長住麼	*ní yào chang djù mo?* nee yow chang joo mo?
I shall stay a few days	我住幾天	*ó djù gĭ tien* o joo gee tee'en
I want to have a wash	我要洗臉	*ó yào hsí lién* o yow shee lee'en
I want something to eat	我要吃點東西	*ó yào chĭh díen dung hsi* o yow chirr dee'en dung shee
anything will do	隨便甚麼東西都可以	*sūi bìen shèn mo dung hsi du kó ĭ* sway bee'en shun mo dung shee doo ko ee
a decanter of water	拏一瓶冷水來	*nā ĭh pīng lĕng shúi lāi* na ee ping lung shway li
give me the key of my room	拏我房間的鑰匙給我	*nā ó fāng gien dy yōh chī gĭh ó* na o fang gee'en dee yo chirr gee o
what are the hours for meals here?	在這裏幾點鐘開飯	*dzài djè lĭ gĭ dién djung kai fàn?* dzi jeh lee gee dee'en jung ki fan?
luncheon is at... and dinner at...	中飯…開,晚飯…開	*djung fàn...kai, wán fàn...kai* jung fan...ki, wan fan...ki

English	Chinese	*Romanized* Pronunciation
There is no fixed time	沒有一定的時候	*mūh yú ĭh dìng dy shĭ hòu* moo yeeoo ee ding dee shirr hou
and breakfast?	早飯幾點鐘	*dzáo fàn gí dién djung?* dzow fan gee dee'en jung?
you can suit your own convenience	你可以隨便吃	*ní kó í sūi bìen chĭh* nee ko ee sway bee'en chirr
can I dine in my room?	我要在房裏吃可以不可以	*ó yào dzai fāng lí chĭh kó í bùh kó í* o yow dzi fang lee chirr ko ee boo ko ee?
are the beds well-aired?	鋪蓋曬過了沒有	*pu gài shài gò liáo mūh yú?* poo ghi shi go leeow moo yeeoo?
where is the w.c.?	廁所在那裏	*szĭ só dzài ná lí?* siz so dzi nah lee?
I suppose you have baths here?	這裏有浴房麼	*dje lí yú yüh fang mo?* jeh lee yoo yeu fang mo?
I want a warm bath	我要洗熱水澡	*ó yào hsí rèh shúi dzáo* o yow shee reh shway dzow
give me some soap	拏肥皂來給我	*nā fēi dzào lāi gíh ó* na fay dzow li gee o
give me a towel	給我洗澡手巾	*gíh ó hsí dzáo shóu gin* gee o shee dzow shou gin
where is the bell?	電鈴在那裏	*dièn līng dzài ná lí?* dee'en ling dzi nah lee?
can you lend me some slippers?	借一雙拖鞋給我	*dzie ĭh shwang to hsiai gíh ó* jeeay ee shwang toh shi gee o
I want a candle	我要一枝蠟燭	*ó yào ĭh djĭ làh djuh* o yow ee jirr la joo
I think of leaving to-morrow	我想明天要走	*ó hsiáng mīng tien yào dzóu* o sheeang ming tee'en yow dzou
call me early in the morning	明天一早叫醒我	*mīng tien ĭh dzáo giao hsing ó* ming tee'en ee dzow geeow shing o
it is chilly to-night	今天晚上很冷	*gin tien wán shàng hěn léng* gin tee'en wan-shang hun lung

English	Chinese	Romanized Pronunciation
Put on more bed-clothes	床上要加一點衣裳	*chwāng shàng yào gia īh diĕn i shāng* chwang shang yow geeah ee dee'en ee shang
send "Boots" to me	叫伺候我們房間的人到這裏來	*giào tsī hou o men fang gien dy rēn dao dje lĭ lāi* geeow tsz hou o mun fang gee'en dee run dow jeh lee li
what do you require, sir?	先生要甚麼	*hsien-seng yào shèn mo ?* shee'en-sung yow shun mo?
give me some hot water	拏一點熱水	*nā īh diĕn rèh shúi* nah ee dee'en reh shway
clean my shoes	刷我的鞋子	*shwah ó dy hsīai-dzī* shwa o dee shi-dz
I want a shave	我要剃鬍子	*ó yào tì hū-dzī* o yow tee hoo-dz
is there a barber about here?	這裏有光臉的麼	*dje lĭ yú gwang liĕn dy mo?* jeh lee yoo gwang lee'en dee mo?
send my boots to be repaired	送我的鞋去補一補	*sùng ó dy hsīai chü bú ih bú* sung o dee shi cheu boo ee boo
let this linen go to the laundry	送這個衣裳到洗衣店去	*sùng djè gò i shāng dào hsi i dien chü* sung jeh go ee shang dow shee ee dee'en cheu
my clothes are wet	我的衣裳濕了	*ó dy i shāng shīh liáo* o dee ee shang shirr leeow
please dry them	你可以拏去烘乾	*ni kó i nā chü hung gan* nee ko ee nah cheu hung gan
brush my clothes	刷我的衣裳	*shwah ó dy i shāng* shwa o dee ee shang
are you going to change your clothes, sir?	先生要換衣裳麼	*hsien seng yào hwan i shāng mo?* shee'en sung yow hwan ee shang mo?

English	Chinese	Romanized Pronunciation
Let us have the bill	拏賬來	*nā djàng lai* nah jang li
is the luggage ready?	行李預備好了麼	*hsīng lì yü bèi hǎo liáo mo?* shing lee yeu bay how leeow mo?
send the luggage to the station	先將行李送到火車站	*hsien dziang hsīng lì sùng dào hǒ che djan* shee'en jeeang shing lee sung dow ho cheh jan
take me to the station	送我到火車站	*sùng ǒ dào hǒ che djan* sung o dow ho cheh jan

Meals

(See Vocabulary pages 37-41.)

飲 食

English	Chinese	Romanized Pronunciation
Show me the bill of fare	拏菜單來給我看	*nā tsài dan lāi gih ǒ kàn* nah tsi dan li gee o kan
please bring tea and cakes	拏茶點來	*nā chā diěn lāi* nah chah dee'en li
what is your order?	先生吩咐要甚麼	*hsien seng fen fù yào shèn mo?* shee'en sung fun foo yow shun mo?
please make me some tea	給我泡茶	*gih ǒ pào chā* gee o pow chah
I will make the tea myself	拏開水我自己泡茶	*nā kai shúi ǒ dzï gi pào chā* nah ki shway o dz gee pow chah
I am hungry	我要吃飯	*ǒ yào chǐh fàn* o yow chirr fan
I am thirsty	我渴了	*ǒ kǒh liáo* o ko leeow

English	Chinese	Romanized Pronunciation
It is quite uneat-able	這個吃不得	*djè gò chĭh bùh dĕh* jeh go chirr boo deh
—undrinkable	這個喝不得	*djè gò hŏh bùh dĕh* jeh go ho boo deh
this is quite enough	這個彀了	*djè gò gòu liáo* jeh go gou leeow
may I offer you some fish?	我拏魚來給先生麼	*ó nā yü̂ lâi gĭh hsien seng mo?* o nah yeu li gee shee'en sung mo?
thanks, I will take some	謝謝,可以拏一點來	*hsie hsie, kó ì nā ĭh dién lâi* sheeay sheeay, ko ee nah ee dee'en li
I am not fond of potatoes	我不喜歡山芋	*ó bùh hsì hwan shan yú* o boo shee hwan shan yeu
it looks tasty	看着好像是好吃	*kàn djoh háo hsiàng shì háo chĭh* kan jo how sheeang shirr how chirr
which do you prefer?	你喜歡那一樣	*nì hsì hwan nà ih yàng?* nee shee hwan na ee yang?
I prefer roast to boiled	我看烤的比燉的好	*ó kàn káo dy bì dùn dy háo* o kan kow dee bee dun dee how
either will do	兩樣皆可	*liáng yàng giai kó* leeang yang geei ko
I have nothing to eat	這裏我沒有的吃	*djè lì o mŭh yù dy chĭh* jay lee o moo yeeoo dee chirr
is the soup ready?	湯好了麼	*tang háo liáo mo?* tang how leeow mo?
dinner is ready (served)	已經開了飯	*ì ging kai liáo fàn* ee ging ki leeow fan
do you like...?	你可喜歡…	*nì kó hsì hwan...?* nee ko shee hwan...?
I must have them fresh	我要新鮮的	*ó yào hsin hsien dy* o yow shin she'een dee
give me a little, please	給我一點	*gĭh ó ĭh dién* gee o ee dee'en

English	Chinese	Romanized Pronunciation
There is none left	都完了	*du wān liáo* doo wan leeow
will you pass the mustard?	請你遞芥末給我	*chǐng nǐ di gìai mūh gih ó* ching nee dee geei mo gee o
another cup of tea	還要一杯茶	*hwān yào ih bei cha* hwan yow ee bay cha
give me some more sugar (milk)	還給我一點白糖(牛奶)	*hāi gih ó ih di'en bēh tāng (niu nái)* hi gee o ee dee'en beh tang (neeoo ni)
put some more water in the teapot	茶壺加一點水	*chā hū gia īh diēn shúi* cha hoo geeah ee dee'en shway
bring me the tea-pot	茶壺拏來	*chā hū nā lāi* cha hoo na li
have you any fresh butter?	有新鮮的奶油麼	*yú hsin hsien dy nái yū mo?* you shin shee'en dee ni yeeoo mo?
what fish have you?	有甚麼樣的魚	*yú shèn mo yàng dy yü* yeeoo shun mo yang dee yeu?
I will take some fish	我要一點魚	*ó yào ih dién yü* o yow ee dee'en yeu
waiter, some bread	侍者帶麵包來	*shī dje, dài mien bao lāi* shirr jay, di mee'en bow li
what wine will you take, sir?	先生喝甚麼酒	*hsien seng hōh shen mo dziu* shee'en sung ho shun mo jeeoo
open the bottle and bring it here	開了缾就拏來	*kāi liáo piñg dziú nā lāi* ki leeow ping jeeoo na li
show me the wine list	酒單拏來給我看	*dziu dan nā lāi gih ó kàn* jeeoo dan na li gee o kan
have you English beer?	有英國皮酒麼	*yú Yīng gwoh pī dziu mo?* yeeoo Ying gwo pee jeeoo mo?
what meat is there?	有甚麼樣的肉	*yú shèn mo yàng dy rùh* yeeoo shun mo yang dee roo
give me a slice of ham	帶一塊火腿來	*dài ih kwài hó túi lai* di ee kwi ho tway li
have you any roast beef?	有烤的牛肉沒有	*yú káo dy niū ruh muh yú* yeeoo kao dee neeoo roo moo yeeoo

English	Chinese	Romanized Pronunciation
Do you prefer well-done or under-done?	你喜歡肉老點是嫩點	*ni hsi hwan rùh láo diĕn, shï nwèn diĕn* nee shee hwan roo low dee'en, shirr nun dee'en
what will you take now?	先生現在要吃甚麼	*hsien seng hsien dzài yào chïh shèn mo?* shee'en sung shee'en dzi yow chirr shun mo?
a little of the fat	拏一點肥的來	*nā ïh diĕn fĕi dy lāi* na ee dee'en fay dee li
give me some lean	給我一點瘦的	*gih ó ïh diĕn sòu dy* gee o ee dee'en sou dee
pass me the sauce	醬油給我	*dziang yū gih ó* jeeang yeeoo gee o
will you carve that fowl?	請你先生分開鷄子	*ching ni hsien seng fen kai gi-dzï* cheeng nee shee'en sung fun ki gee-dz
change my plate	換一個盤子	*hwàn ïh gò pān-dzï* hwan ee go pan-dz
will you have some potatoes?	山芋要不要	*shan-yü yào bùh yáo* shan yeu yow boo yow
boiled potatoes	煮的山芋	*dju dy shan yü* joo dee shan yeu
roasted potatoes	烤的山芋	*kào dy shan yü* kow dee shan yeu
hand me your plate	盤子遞給我	*pān-dzï dì gih ó* pan-dz dee gee o
I will not take any	我不要了	*ó bùh yào liáo* o boo yow leeow
I should like some buttered toast	我要一點烘麵包加奶油	*ó yào ïh diĕn hung mien bao gia nài yū* o yow ee dee'en hung mee'en bow geeah ni yeeoo
shall I bring you some more?	我還拏一點給你好不好	*ó hāi nā ïh diĕn gih ni háo bùh háo?* o hi nah ee dee'en gee nee how boo how?
No, thank you, I can't eat any more	謝謝不要我不能再吃了	*hsìe, hsìe, bùh yào, ó bùh nĕng dzài chïh liáo* sheeay sheeay boo yow, o boo nung dzi chirr leeow

The Time

(See Vocabulary pages 26-28.)

NOTE.—(1) The Chinese say "twenty minutes to four," or "a quarter to six," as in English but also frequently state the minutes past the hour. For example, "twenty minutes to four" is expressed as "forty minutes past three," and "a quarter to six" "three quarters past five."

(2) A.M. is expressed by prefixing the word "shang-woo," and P.M. by the word "sheeah-woo" for afternoon and "yea" for night.

English	Chinese	*Romanized* Pronunciation
What time is it?	幾點鐘	*gī diĕn djung?* gee dee'en jung?
it is eight o'clock	八點鐘	*bàh dien djung* ba dee'en jung
half-past nine	九點半鐘	*gīu diĕn bàn djung* geeoo dee'en ban jung
a quarter to twelve	十一點三刻鐘	*shih īh dien san kèh djung* shirr ee dee'en san keh jung
twenty minutes past one	一點過二十分	*īh diĕn go èr shīh fen* ee dee'en go ur shirr fun
ten minutes to two	兩點少十分	*liăng dien shao shīh fen* leeang dee'en show shirr fun
a quarter past four	四點一刻	*szi diĕn īh kèh* siz dee'en ee keh
it is just about noon	將近正午	*dziang gin djeng wŭ* jee'ang gin jung woo
10 a.m	上午十點鐘	*shàng wŭ shīh diĕn djung* shang woo shirr dee'en jung
11 p.m.	夜裏十一點鐘	*yè lī shīh īh diĕn djung* yeh lee shirr ee dee'en jung
it commences at half-past one	一點半鐘開	*īh diĕn bàn djung kai* ee dee'en ban jung ki
I will come to-morrow	我明天來	*ó mīng tien lāi* o ming tee'en li

English	Chinese	*Romanized* Pronunciation
Early in the morning	清早	*ching dzǎo* ching dzow
it is now late	已經晚了	*ǐ ging wan liǎo* ee ging wan leeow
every other day	隔一天	*kěh ih tien* keh ee tee'en
day after to-morrow	後天	*hòu tien* hou tee'en
day before yesterday	前天	*tsien tien* chee'en tee'en
half-an hour	半點鐘	*bàn diěn djung* ban dee'en jung
an hour and a half	一點半鐘	*īh diěn bàn djung* ee dee'en ban jung
for a short time	一霎時	*īh shah shī* ee shah shirr
at any time	隨時	*sūi shī* sway shirr
at the same time	同一個時候	*tūng īh go shī hòu* tung ee go shirr hou

The Weather

(For Vocabularies see pages 14, 15, 26.)

天 氣

English	Chinese	*Romanized* Pronunciation
It is fine weather	天氣好	*tien chi hǎo* tee'en chee how
it is most disagreeable weather	天氣頂壞	*tien chi ding hwai* tee'en chee ding hwi
it is really beautiful weather	天氣實在好	*tien chi shǐh dzai hǎo* tee'en chee shirr dzi how

English	Chinese	Romanized Pronunciation
I am knocked up by this heat	熱的要命	*rèh dy yào mìng* reh dee yow ming
the heat is unbearable to-day	今天熱的受不住	*gin tien rèh dy shòu bùh djù* gin tee'en reh dee shou boo joo
it is terribly hot	今天熱的可怕	*gin tee'en rèh dy kó pà* gin tee'en reh dee ko pah
I will come tomorrow if fine	明天天好我就來	*mīng tee'en, tee'en háo ó dzìu lāi* ming tee'en, tee'en how o jeeoo li
can you lend me an umbrella?	可能借一把洋傘給我麼	*kó nēng dzie īh bá yāng sán gīh ó mo?* ko nung jeeay ee bah yang san gee o mo?
is it raining?	下雨麼	*hsìa yü mo?* sheeah yeu mo?
it is raining a little	下小雨	*hsìa hsiáo yü* sheeah sheeow yeu
it looks as if the rain would clear off	看天這樣是要晴了	*kàn tien djè yàng shì yào dzīng liáo* kan tee'en jay yang shirr yow jing leeow
we were (*or*, I was) kept in by the rain	因爲下雨我們(我)不能出來	*yin wèi hsìa yü ó-mēn (ó) bùh nēng chùh lāi* yin way sheeah yeu o-mun (o) boo nung choo li
it seems likely to rain	看天似乎是要下雨	*kàn tien szì hu shì yào hsìa yü* kan tee'en siz hoo shirr yow sheeah yeu
it is snowing	下了雪	*hsìa liáo hsüeh* sheeah leeow sheueh

Health

(See Vocabulary pages 35, &c.)

衞生

English	Chinese	Romanized Pronunciation
I feel ill	我不受用	*ó bùh shòu yùng* o boo shou yung
I have a sore throat	喉嚨疼	*hōu lūng tēng* hou lung tung
I have a headache	頭疼	*tōu tēng* tou tung
I have caught cold	傷了風	*shang liáo feng* shang leeow fung
I have a pain in my back	腰疼	*yao tēng* yow tung
I have a bad cough	我很咳嗽	*ó hén kèh sù* o hun keh sou
I have a pain here	我這個地方疼	*ó djë gò dì fang tēng* o jeh go dee fang tung
you had better consult the doctor	你不如請醫生看罷	*ní bùh rū tsíng i seng kàn bà* nee boo roo cheeng ee sung kan bah
please call a good doctor for me	請你替我請一個好醫生	*tsíng ní tì ó tsíng ih go háo i seng* ching nee tee o ching ee go how ee sung
he will come immediately	他立刻要來	*ta lih kèh yào lāi* tah lee keh yow li
the doctor has come	醫生來了	*i seng lāi liáo* ee sung li leeow
I wish to consult you	請你看我的病	*tsíng ní kàn ó dy bìng* ching nee kan o dee bing
let me feel your pulse	我替你把脈	*ó tì ní bá mèh* o tee nee bah meh

English	Chinese	Romanized Pronunciation
How do you feel to-day?	你今天好些麼	*ni gin tien hǎo hsie mo?* nee gin tee'en how sheeay mo?
much better, thanks	謝謝你,我今天好些	*hsìe hsìe nì, ó gin tien hǎo hsie* sheeay sheeay nee, o gin tee'en how sheeay
have it made up at a chemist's	這個叫藥店裏替你配	*djè go giao yoh dìen lì tì nì pèi* jeh go geeow yo dee'en lee tee nee pay
where is there a chemist's shop?	藥店在那裏	*yōh dìen dzai nǎ lì?* yo dee'en dzi nah lee?
here is the medicine	藥在這裏	*yōh dzai djè lì* yo dzi jeh lee
this medicine is to be taken three times a day	這個藥一天敷三次	*djè gò yōh ih tien fu san tsì* jeh go yo ee tee'en foo san tsz

Correspondence. The Post-office. Telegrams

(See Vocabularies pages 79, &c.)

信 件 電 則

English	Chinese	Romanized Pronunciation
Have no letters come this morning?	今早沒有來信麼	*gin dzǎo mūh yú lāi hsin mo?* gin dzow moo yeeoo li shin mo?
no, none have come	沒有	*mūh yú* moo yeeoo
I have not received a letter (letters)	我沒有收到信	*ó mūh yú shou dào hsin* o moo yeeoo shou dow shin

English	Chinese	*Romanized* Pronunciation
Please post this letter	請你拏這封信寄去	*tsing ni nā djè feng hsin gi chü* ching nee nah jeh fung shin gee cheu
he ought to be here by now	這個時候該到了	*djè gò shī hòu gai dào liao* jeh go shirr hou ghi dow leeow
I have heard nothing	我沒有聽見甚麼信息	*ó mūh yú ting gien shèn mo hsin hsih* o moo yeeoo ting gee'en shun mo shin shee
has the mail steamer arrived?	信船到了沒有	*hsin chwān dào liáo mūh yú?* shin chwan dow leeow moo yeeoo?
go and see if the mail is (letters are) in	你去看信來了沒有	*ni chü kàn hsin lāi liao mūh yú* nee cheu kan shin li leeow moo yeeoo
are there any letters for me?	有我的信沒有	*yú ó dy hsin mūh yù?* yoo o dee shin moo yeeoo
please forward my letters to...	請將我的信寄到…	*tsing dziang ó dy hsin gi dào...* ching jeeang o dee shin gee dow...
please weigh this letter (these letters)	請替我戥這個(些)信	*tsing ti ó deng djè gò (hsie) hsin* ching tee o dung jeh go (sheeay) shin
how much is the postage on this letter (these letters)?	這個(些)信的郵費多少	*djè gò (hsie) hsin dy yu fèi do sháo?* jeh go (sheeay) shin dee yeeoo fay doh show?
this letter is to be registered	這個信要掛號	*djè gò hsin yào gwa hào* jeh go shin yow gwah how
receipt for registered letter	這是掛號信的收條	*dje shī gwa hào hsin dy shou tiāo* jeh shirr gwah how shin dee shou teeow

English	Chinese	*Romanized* Pronunciation
A registered letter	掛號信	*gwa hào hsin* gwah how shin
I am just going to read it	我馬上要看	*ó má shàng yào kàn* o mah shang yow kan
tell him to wait	叫他等一等	*gìao ta déng ih déng* geeow tah dung ee dung
I will send a reply later	後來要寄回信	*hòu lāi yào gi hwēi hsin* hou li yow gee hway shin
can I send a telegram?	我可以打電報麼	*ó kó ì dá dìen bào mo?* o ko ee dah dee'en bow mo?
I have received a telegram from...	我收了...來的電報	*ó shou liáo...lāi dy dìen bào* o shou leeow...li dee dee'en-bow
has a telegram come for me?	有我的電報麼	*yú ó dy dìen bào mo?* yeeoo o dee'en bow mo?
please send this telegram	請將這個電報寄去	*tsing dziang djè gò dìen bào gi chü* ching jeeang jay go dee'en bow gee cheu
I want a postal order	我要買一張匯票	*ó yào mái ìh djang hwei pìao* o yow mi ee jang hway peeow
the payee's name and address is...	收票人的姓名住址是...	*shou pìao rēn dy hsing mīng dju djī shī...* shou peeow run dee shing ming joo jirr shirr...
the sender's name and address is...	寄票人的姓名住址是...	*gi pìao rēn dy hsing mīng dju djī shī...* gee peeow run dee shing ming joo jirr shirr...
I am the sender	我就是寄票人	*ó dziu shī gi pìao rēn* o jeeoo shirr gee peeow run
please cash this money-order (postal-order)	請你將這個匯票的錢給我	*tsing nǐ dziang djè gò hwei pìao dy chīen gíh ó* ching nee jeeang jay go hway peeow dee chee'en gee o

CONVERSATIONS

Introductions

NOTE.—To "introduce" a person in Chinese generally means to present that person to one likely to be a patron politically or otherwise.

舉 薦

English	Chinese	Romanized Pronunciation
This is Mr.... allow me to introduce you	這是……先生請你們兩下會會	*dje shï...Hsien seng, tsing nǐ mēn liang hsia hwèi hwèi* jeh shirr......Shee'en sung, ching nee mun leeang sheeah hway hway
kindly give me a letter of introduction to Mr....	請你寫一封薦書給我我去見…先生	*tsing nǐ hsiě īh feng gìen shu gǐh ǒ, o chü gien...Hsien seng* cheeng nee sheeay ee feng gee'en shoo gee o, o cheu gee'en...Shee'en sung
here is the letter of introduction to him	這是給先生的薦書	*dje shï gǐh Hsien seng dy gìen shu* jeh shirr gee Shee'en sung dee gee'en shoo
allow me to introduce myself to you; my name is...	我特來會先生我的姓名是……	*ǒ tèh lái hwei Hsien seng, ǒ dy sìng mìng shï...* o teh li hway Shee'en sung, o dee shing ming shirr...
please introduce me to Mr....	請你薦我到……先生那裏	*tsing nǐ gìen ǒ dào...Hsien seng nà lǐ* ching nee gee'en o dow... Shee'en sung nah lee
I beg to introduce Mr...., a friend of mine	這是……先生他是我的朋友我要薦給你	*dje shï...Hsien seng, ta shï ǒ dy pěng yú, ǒ yào gìer gǐh nǐ* jeh shirr...Shee'en sung, tah shirr o dee pung yeeoo, o yow gee'en gee nee
here is my card	這是我的粗柬	*dje shï ǒ dy tsu gién* jeh shirr o dee tsoo gee'en
pleased to make your acquaintance	旣得相聚很妙很妙	*gì dèh hsiang dzü hěn mìao hěn mìao* gee deh sheeang dzeu hun meeow hun meeow

English	Chinese	*Romanized* Pronunciation
I trust you will honour me with your continued friendship	得蒙長遠不棄是爲我心所願	*dèh mēng chang yüén bùh chi shī wēi ó hsin só yüen* deh mung chang yeuehn boo chee shirr way o shin so yeuehn
I will call again	改日再來拜會	*gái rïh dzai lāi bài hwei* gh**i** rirr dz**i** l**i** b**i** hway

In Town; Visiting

(See Vocabulary, pages 29-32.)

NOTE.—For hiring conveyances see "Travelling by Road," p. 115. See also "Enquiries," p. 109 and "Shopping," p. 141.

城 內 拜 客

English	Chinese	*Romanized* Pronunciation
What shall we do?	我們要作甚麼事	*ó mēn yào dzo shèn mo szï?* o mun yow dzo shun mo siz?
very well; come along	很好,可以走罷	*hén háo, ko i dzóu ba* hun how, ko ee dzou bah
am I wrong to have come at this time?	我現在來的不便嗎	*ó hsìen dzài lāi dy bùh lìe ma?* o shee'en dz**i** l**i** dee boo bee'en ma?
excuse my having kept you waiting	得罪你叫你等了許久	*dèh dzui ní, giào ní dèng liáo hsü gíu* deh dzway nee, geeow nee dung leeow sheu geeoo
you wait here	你在這裏等等	*ní dzái dje lí déng déng* nee dz**i** jeh lee dung dung
suppose we go?	我們可以去罷	*ó mēn kó i chü bà?* o mun ko ee cheu bah?

English	Chinese	*Romanized* Pronunciation
I am tired; let us rest a little	我疲倦了歇歇罷	*ó pi güén líao, hsieh hsieh ba* o pee geuehn leeow, shee'eh shee'eh bah
I am tired out	哎喲累倒了	*aì-yà, lèi dao liáo* ī yah, lay dow leeow
take care! (look out!)	當心當心	*dang hsin, dang hsin* dang shin, dang shin
take care of yourself!	你招呼自己要當心	*ní djao hu dzï gí yào dang hsin* nee jow hoo dz gee yow dang shin
I say! (Hallo there!)	噯,同你說話	*aì, tūng ní shwoh hwa* ī, tung nee shwo hwah
where are you going?	你到那裏去	*ní dào ná lí chü?* nee dow nah lee cheu?
I am going out now for a walk	現在我出去逛逛	*hsìen dzài ó chùh chü gwang gwang* shee'en dzī o choo cheu gwang gwang
I should like to accompany you	我要同你一陣去	*ó yào tūng ní īh djen chü* o yow tung nee ee jun cheu
I was waiting for you	我等你	*ó deng ní* o dung nee
I was just going out	我正要出去	*ó djèng yào chùh chu* o jung yow choo cheu
I shall walk as far as the post-office	我要走到信局那裏	*ó yào dzou dào hsin güh nà lí* o yow dzou dow shin geu nah lee
I will wait until this evening	好,我等到今天晚上	*hao! ó déng dào gin tien wán shàng* how! o dung dow gin tee'en wan shang
wait till I come	等我來	*déng ó lāi* dung o lī
I cannot come	我不得來	*ó bùh dèh lāi* o boo deh lī
I am in a hurry	我忙得很	*ó māng dèh hěn* o mang deh hun

English	Chinese	*Romanized* Pronunciation
Be quick!	你快些	*ní kwai hsie* nee kwi sheeay
what a grand sight!	實在好看	*shīh dzai háo kàn* shirr dzi how kan
we needn't hurry	不要慌	*bùh yào hwang* boo yow hwang
now I am at leisure	現在我有空了	*hsien dzai ó yú kùng liáo* shee'en dzi o yeeoo kung leeow
kindly wait a little	請你等一刻	*tsíng ní déng īh kèh* ching nee dung ee keh
I will not wait	我不等	*ó bùh déng* o boo dung
I have come to borrow a hammer	我來借一個釘鎚	*ó lāi dzie ih gò ding chūi* o li jeeay ee go ding chway
I will send it back to-morrow	明天送回來	*mīng tien sùng hwēī lāi* ming tee'en sung hway li
we were just speaking about you	我們剛纔說到你	*ó mēn gang tsái shwoh dào ní* o mun gang tsi shwo dow nee
go and tell him to be sure and come	你去告訴他一定要來	*ní chü gào sù ta īh dìng yàó lāi* nee cheu gow soo tah ee ding yow li
I have lost my way	我迷失了路	*ó mī shīh liáo lù* o mee shirr leeow loo
direct me to...	請你指我到...	*tsíng ní djī ó dào...* cheeng nee jirr o dow...
take the first turning to the right	走到第一個十字路向右手轉灣	*dzóu dào dì īh gò shīh dzī lù, hsiàng yù shòu djwán wan* dzou dow dee ee go shirr dz loo, sheeang yeeoo shou jwan wan
take the second turning to the left	走到第二個十字路向左手轉灣	*dzou dào dì èr gò shīh dzī lù, hsiang dzo shóu djwán wan* dzou dow dee ur go shirr dz loo, sheeang dzo shou jwan wan

English	Chinese	Romanized Pronunciation
It is right in front of you	就在你面前	*dziu dzai ni mien tsien* jeeoo dzi nee mee'en chee'en
this is the shortest way	這條路近些	*dje tiao lù gìn hsie* jeh teeow loo gin sheeay
this is the longest way	這條路遠些	*dje tiao lù yüěn hsie* jeh teeow loo yeuehn sheeay
it is straight on	一直朝前	*ih djih djao tsien* ee jirr jow chee'en
I will show you his place	我給你看他的地方	*ó gih ni kàn ta dy dì fang* o gee nee kan tah dee dee fang
it is only five minutes' walk	五分鐘可以走到	*wú fen djung kó i dzóu dào* woo fun jung ko ee dzou dow
I don't know anyone of that name	這個人的名子我不認得	*djè gò rēn dy mīng dz ó bùh rèn dèh* jeh go run dee ming dz o boo run deh
I dont know where he lives	不曉得他在那裏住	*bùh hsiao deh tā dzài nǎ li dju* boo sheeow deh tah dzi nah lee joo
is your master (mistress) within?	主人(太太)在家麼	*dju rēn (tài-tài) dzài gia mo?* joo run (ti-ti) dzi geeah mo?
no, has gone out	不在家出去了	*bùh dzài gia; chùh chü liáo* boo dzi geeah; choo cheu leeow
is Mrs. ...at home?	…太太在家麼	*...tài-tài dzai gia mo?* ...ti-ti dzi geeah mo?
let your master know I have come	你對主人說我來過了	*ni dùi dju rēn shwoh ó lāi gò liao* nee dway joo run shwo o li go leeow
you had better go and ask	你不如去問罷	*ni bùh rū chü wèn bà* nee boo roo cheu wun bah
he is at home	他在家	*ta dzài gia* tah dzi geeah

English	Chinese	*Romanized* Pronunciation
Please come in	請你進來	*tsing ni dzin lāi* ching nee dzin lī
take a seat for a minute	請坐一刻	*tsing dzò īh kèh* ching dzo ee keh
who has come?	那一個來的	*ná īh gò lāi dy?* nah ee go lī dee?
has someone come?	有人來了麼	*yú rēn lāi liáo mo?* yeeoo run lī leeow mo?
a visitor has come, sir	來了一位客	*lāi liáo īh wèi kèh* lī leeow ee way keh
show him (her) in	請他進來	*tsíng ta dzin lāi* ching tah dzin lī
really it is an age since we last met	久違久違	*giú wēi, giú wāy* geeoo way, geeoo way
excuse my leaving first	得罪你我少陪了	*dèh dzui ni, ó sháo pēi liáo* deh dzway nee, o show pay leeow
I have been so busy that I could not come and see you	我很忙不得空過來拜候	*ó hěn māng; bùh dèh kùng gò lāi bài hòu* o hen mang; boo deh kung go lī bī hou
I must go now	我要走了	*ó yào dzou liào* o yow dzou leeow
must you really go?	一定要去嗎	*īh dìng yào chü mo?* ee ding yow cheu mo?
remember me to all at home	請代我問候府上	*tsing dài ó wèn hòu fú shàng* ching dī o wun hou foo shang
go slowly! (to departing guest)	慢慢走	*màn-màn dzóu* man man dzou
good bye!	再會	*dzài hwèi* dzī hway
please come again	請便中再來	*tsing bien djung dzài lāi* ching bee'en jung dzī lī
did anyone call while I was out?	我不在家有人來了沒有	*ó bùh dzài gia yú rēn lāi liáo mūh yú?* o boo dzī geeah yeeoo run lī leeow moo yeeoo?

English	Chinese	Romanized Pronunciation
A visitor came just as you left	你纔出門的時候來了一位客	*ní tsāi chūh mēn dy shī hòu lāi liáo īh wèi kèh* nee tsi choo mun dee shirr hou li leeow ee way keh
I am glad I went	幸虧我去了	*hsing kwei ó chū liáo* shing kway o cheu leeow

Shopping

(See Vocabularies, pages 17, 25, 37, 41, etc.)

買 賣

English	Chinese	Romanized Pronunciation
I want some silk	我要買綢子	*ó yào mái chōu-dz* o yow mi chou dz
this silk is very dear	這個綢子很貴	*djè gò chōu-dz hĕn gwèi* jeh go chou dz hun gway
this material wears well	這個料經穿	*djè gò liao ging chwan* jeh go leeow ging chwan
I will guarantee i	我可以包用	*ó kó ī bao yùng* o ko ee bow yung
I don't guarantee it	那我不能包用	*nà ó bùh nēng bao yùng* nah o boo nung bow yung
please show me some gloves	請拏手套給我看	*tsing nā shóu tào gih ó kàn* ching nah shou tow gee o kan
how much is this cabinet?	這個櫃子多少錢	*dje gò gwei-dz do sháo tsien?* jeh go gway dz doh show chee'en?
may I see it?	給我看看嗎	*gih ó kàn kàn ma?* gee o kan kan mah?
I want to see that screen	我要看看那個屏風	*ó yào kàn kàn nò gò pīng feng* o yow kan kan nah go ping fung

English	Chinese	*Romanized* Pronunciation
I should think it would do	我想可以用了	*ó hsiáng kó ĭ yùng liáo* o sheeang ko ee yung leeow
what is the lowest price?	頂便宜要甚麽價錢	*díng pīen ī yào shèn mo gìa tsīen?* ding pee'en ee yow shun mo geeah chee'en
is this vase expensive?	這個花絣貴不貴	*djè gò hwa pīng gwèi bùh gwèi?* jeh go hwah ping gway boo gway?
I will select the best from among these	我要揀一個頂好的	*ó yào gíen ĭh gò díng háo dy* o yow gee'en ee go ding how dee
may I choose for myself?	我可自己揀麽	*ó kó dzï gí gién mo?* o ko dz gee gee'en mo?
may I show it to you?	我可以拏來給你看看	*ó kó ĭ nā lāi gíh ní kàn kàn* o ko ee na lī gee nee kan kan
please give me about ten	給我十來個	*gíh ó shĭh la gò* gee o shirr lah go
this suits me, but the price is too high	這個很好但是價錢太貴	*djè gò hén háo, dàn shī gìa tsīen tài gwei* jeh go hun how, dan shirr geeah chee'en tī gway
it is not new	這不是新的	*djè bùh shī hsin dy* jeh boo shirr shin dee
I don't want any more	多的我不要	*do dy ó bùh yào* doh dee o boo yow
I have ordered it	我已經定了	*ó ĭ gìng dìng liao* o ee ging ding leeow
it's (dearer cheaper) than I thought	比我想的貴(便宜)些	*bí ó hsiáng dy gwèi (pīen-ī) hsie* bee o sheeang dee gway (pee'en ee) sheeay
this is native made	這是本地作的	*djè shī bén dì dzo dy* jeh shirr bun dee dzo dee
that is imported	那是外路來的	*nà shī wài lù lāi dy* nah shirr wī loo lī dee

English	Chinese	Romanized Pronunciation
This is a still better one	這是一個更好的	*dje shï ïh gó gèng háo dy* jeh shirr ee go gung how dee
it won't do at all	這個不中用	*dje gò bùh djung yùng* jeh go boo jung yung
I must have it	我定準要	*ó dìng djwen yào* o ding jwun yow
how much do you require?	你要多少	*ní yào do sháo?* nee yow doh show?
I will buy these	我要買這個	*ó yào mái djè gò* o yow mi jeh go
how do you like these?	這些好不好	*djè hsíe háo bùh háo?* jeh sheeay how boo how?
I don't like any of these	這些我都不歡喜	*djè hsíe ó du bùh hwan hsí* jay sheeay o doo boo hwan shee
how much do you ask for it?	這些賣甚麼價錢	*dje hsie mái shèn mo gìa tsïen?* jeh sheeay mi shun mo geeah chee'en?
I can't let you have them for less	少了不能賣	*sháo liáo bùh nëng mài* show leeow boo nung mi
are they really genuine?	實在是眞的嗎	*shïh dzài shï djen dy ma?* shirr dzi shirr jun dee mah?
send the things to my hotel	把這個送到客寓去	*bá djè gò sùng dào kèh yü chü* bah jay go sung dow keh yeu cheu

Commercial and Trading

(For Vocabulary see pages 66-78.)

批 發 買 賣

English	Chinese	Romanized Pronunciation
May I show you my samples?	我可以拏樣子給你看看麼	*ó kó ï nä yàng-dz gíh ní kàn kàn mo?* o ko ee nah yang dz gee nee kan kan mo?

English	Chinese	Romanized Pronunciation
I can sell at...	我可以照…錢一件賣給你	*ó kŏ ĭ djao...chīen ĭh gĭen mài gĭh nĭ* o ko ee jow...chee'en ee gee'en mi gee nee
it is impossible to sell at that figure	那個價錢不能賣	*nà gŏ gia tsīen bŭh nĕng mài* nah go geeah chee'en boo nung mi
we will consider the matter	我們斟酌再說	*ó mēn djen djoh dzài shwoh* o mun jun joh dzi shwo
I will consult my partner and let you know	我要問問同事的然後告訴你	*ó yào wèn wèn tūng szī dy rān hòu gào sù nĭ* o yow wun wun tung siz dee ran hou gow soo nee
I don't think my partner would consent to trade at that price	我想我的同事的不肯照這個價錢	*ó hsiáng ó dy tūng szī dy bùh kĕn djao dje gŏ gia tsīen* o sheeang o dee tung siz dee boo kun jow jeh go geeah chee'en
I'm afraid I shall lose on the sale of the goods	這個生意恐怕我是要賠本的	*djè gŏ seng ì kúng pà ó shì yào pēi bén dy* jeh go sung ee kung pah o shirr yow pay bun dee
I will assume the liability	這個事我可以擔保	*dje gŏ szī ó kŏ ĭ dan băo* jeh go siz o ko ee dan bow
I want samples of...	我要看看…的樣子	*ó yào kàn kàn...dy yàng-dz* o yow kan kan...dee yang-dz
I want some samples	請給我幾個樣子看	*tsíng gĭh ó gĭ gŏ yàng-dz kàn* ching gee o gee go yang dz kan
we have none in stock	店裏沒有	*dĭen lĭ mŭh yú* dee'en lee moo yeeoo
the goods are inferior to sample	這個貨不如樣子了	*dje gŏ hŏ bùh rū yàng-dz liáo* jeh go ho boo roo yang dz leeow

English	Chinese	Romanized Pronunciation
Show me several patterns	拏幾個樣子給我看	*nā gí gò yàng-dz gíh ó kàn* na gee go yang dz gee o kan
when can you deliver if I give you an order?	若是定了你到甚麼時候可以交貨	*ròh shī dìng liáo ní dào shèn mo shī hòu kó í giao hò?* ro shirr ding leeow nee dow shun mo shirr hou ko ee geeow ho?
I cannot give you an order	我不能定貨	*ó bùh nēng dìng hò* o boo nung ding ho
I wish to cancel the order	我所定的貨鈎銷了罷	*ó só díng dy hò gou shao liao bà* o so ding dee ho gou show leeow bah
we will consult after receiving samples	收了樣子以後再作商量	*shou liáo yàng-dz í hóu dzai dzoh shang liang* shou leeow yang dz ee hou dzi dzo shang leeang
you must come down a great deal	你總要比這個便宜不少了	*ní dzúng yào bí dje gò pīen ī búh sháo liáo* nee dzung yow bee jeh go pee'en ee boo show leeow
I can't come down	不能再便宜了	*bùh nēng dzài pīen ī liáo* boo nung dzi pee'en ee leeow
I can't buy at that figure	這個價錢我不能買了	*dje gò gìa tsīen ó bùh nēng mái liao* jeh go geeah chee'en o boo nung mi leeow
what is your bottom price?	少到底甚麼價錢	*sháo dào di shèn mo gìa tsīen?* show dow dee shun mo geeah chee'en
have the goods shipped at once	馬上拏貨送上船去	*má shàng nā hò sùng shàng chwān chì* ma shang nah ho sung shang chwan cheu
have you shipped the goods?	貨上了船沒有	*hò shàng liao chwān mūh yú?* ho shang leeow chwan moo yeeoo?

English	Chinese	Romanized Pronunciation
These goods must be carefully packed	這些貨要裝的好	*dje hsie hò yào djwang dy háo* jeh sheeay ho yow jwang dee how
put this mark on the boxes	箱子上要寫這個碼子	*hsiang dz shàng yào hsie djè gò má dz* sheeang dz shang yow sheeay jeh go mah dz
the boxes must be tin-lined	箱子裏面要鐵皮	*hsiang dz lí mien yào tieh pi* sheeang dz lee mee'en yow tee'eh pee
trade is dull	生意不好	*seng ì bùh háo* sung ee boo how
trade is good	生意興旺	*seng ì hsing wàng* sung ee shing wang
he has become bankrupt	他的店倒了	*ta dy dìen dáo liáo* tah dee dee'en dow leeow
there are some errors in the account	這個賬不對	*djè gó djàng bùh dùi* jeh go jang boo dway
you have overcharged me	賬上開的錢太多了	*djàng shàng kai dy tsien tài do liao* jang shang ki dee chee'en ti doh leeow
this is a clerical error	這個字是寫錯了	*dje gò dzì shì hsie tso liáo* jeh go dz shirr sheeay tso leeow
I have deducted the errors	多的數目已經去掉了	*do dy sù mùh ì ging chü dìao liáo* doh dee soo moo ee ging cheu deeow leeow
it is more than was arranged	這個賬比所定的價錢多了	*dje gò djang bí só dìng dy gìa tsien do liáo* jeh go jang bee so ding dee geeah chee'en doh leeow
I want a detailed account	要開細賬	*yào kai hsì djàng* yow ki shee jang
here is a cheque for the amount of your account	這個匯票可以把賬還清了	*dje gó hwei pìao ko ì ba djàng hwān ching liao* jeh go hway peeow ko ee ba jang hwan ching liao

English	Chinese	Romanized Pronunciation
Sent in our account	賬已經送你了	*djàng ee ging sùng nee liao* jang ee ging sung nee leeow
will you accept a bill?	我給你匯票可以不可以	*ó gĭh nĭ hwei pìao kó ĭ bùh kó ĭ?* o gee nee hway peeow ko ee boo ko ee?

Changing Money

兌 錢

English	Chinese	Romanized Pronunciation
Where is there a money-changer's?	錢店在那裏	*tsĭen dìen dzài ná lĭ?* chee'en dee'en dzi nah lee?
can you give me change for this?	這個能換麼	*djè gò neng hwàn mo?* jeh go nung hwan mo?
yes, sir; what change do you wish?	可以,先生換甚麼錢	*kó ĭ, Hsien sung hwàn shèn mo tsien?* ko ee, Shee'en sung hwan shun mo chee'en?
will you give me current coin?	給我通用的錢	*gĭh ó tung yung dy tsĭen* gee o tung yung dee chee'en
please give me 10 dollar Bank notes	請你給我十塊錢的票子	*tsĭng nĭ gĭh ó shĭh kwai tsĭen dy pĭao-dz* ching nee gee o shirr kwi chee'en dee peeow dz
give me the amount in dollars	這些就給我洋錢	*dje hsie dziu gĭh ó yāng tsĭen* jeh sheeay jeeoo gee o yang chee'en
change this into small silver money, please	這個換角子	*dje gò hwan gōh-dz* jeh go hwan go dz
change this into copper cents	這個換銅角子	*dje gò hwan tūng gōh-dz* jeh go hwan tung go dz

English	Chinese	*Romanized* Pronunciation
Will you cash this cheque for me?	你能替我換這個匯票麽	*nì nĕng tì ó hwan dje go hwei pìao mo?* nee nung tee o hwan jeh go hway peeow mo?
what is the rate of exchange on English money?	英國的金洋換甚麽價錢	*Ying gwoh dy gin yāng hwan shen mo gìa tsīen* Ying gwo dee gin yang hwan shun mo geeah chee'en?
please change me an English bank-note	這是英國的鈔票請換錢給我	*dje shī Ying gwoh dy chao pìao, tsing hwan tsīen gih ó* jeh shirr Ying gwo dee chow peeow, ching hwan chee'en gee o
a 10 $ Hongkong and Shanghai bank-note	一個匯豐銀行十塊錢的票子	*ih go hwei feng yin hāng shīh kwai ts'ien dy piao-dz* ee go hway feng yin hang shih kwai chee'en dy peeow dz
a cheque	一個匯票	*ĭh gò hwei pìao* ee go hway peeow
a bill of exchange	商用匯票	*shang yùng hwei pìao* shang yung hway peeow
letter of credit	銀行保證書	*yīn hāng bao djeng shu* yin hang bow jung shoo
banker's order	匯銀信	*hwei yīn hsin* hway yin shin
money order (postal)	郵政匯票	*yū djeng hwei pìao* yeeoo jun hway peeow
telegraphic draft	電報匯票	*dièn bǎo hwei pìao* dee'en bow hway peeow

Numerals 數目字

CARDINAL

English	Chinese	*Romanized* Pronunciation	English	Chinese	*Romanized* Pronunciation
1	一	*ih* ee	19	十九	*shĭh giu* shirr geeoo
2	二	*èr* ur	20	二十	*èr shĭh* ur shirr
3	三	*san* san	30	三十	*san shĭh* san shirr
4	四	*szŭ* siz	40	四十	*szŭ shĭh* siz shirr
5	五	*wù* woo	50	五十	*wù shĭh* woo shirr
6	六	*lùh* loo	60	六十	*lùh shĭh* loo shirr
7	七	*tsih* chee	70	七十	*tsih shĭh* chee shirr
8	八	*bah* ba	80	八十	*bah shĭh* bah shirr
9	九	*giu* geeoo	90	九十	*giù shĭh* geeoo shirr
10	十	*shĭh* shirr	100	一百	*ih beh* ee beh
11	十一	*shĭh ih* shirr ee	101	一百零一	*ih beh ling ih* ee beh ling ih
12	十二	*shĭh èr* shirr úr	102	„ „ „ 二	„ „ „ *èr* „ „ „ ur
13	十三	*shĭh san* shirr san	103	„ „ „ 三	„ „ „ *san* „ „ „ san
14	十四	*shĭh szŭ* shirr siz	104	„ „ „ 四	„ „ „ *szŭ* „ „ „ siz
15	十五	*shĭh wù* shirr woo	105	„ „ „ 五	„ „ „ *wù* „ „ „ woo
16	十六	*shĭh lùh* shirr loo	106	„ „ „ 六	„ „ „ *lùh* „ „ „ loo
17	十七	*shĭh tsih* shirr chee	107	„ „ „ 七	„ „ „ *tsih* „ „ „ chee
18	十八	*shĭh bah* shirr ba	108	„ „ „ 八	„ „ „ *bah* „ „ „ ba

English	Chinese	Romanized Pronunciation	English	Chinese	Romanized Pronunciation
109	一百零九	*ih beh ling giù* ee beh ling geeoo	300	三百	*san beh* san beh
110	„ „ 一十	*ih beh ih shĭh* ee beh ee shirr	400	四百	*szï* „ siz „
120	„ „ 二 „	*ih beh ér* ee beh ur	500	五百	*wù* „ woo „
130	„ „ 三	*ih beh san* ee beh san	600	六百	*lúh* „ loo „
140	„ „ 四	*ih beh szï* ee beh siz	700	七百	*tsih* „ chee „
150	„ „ 五	*ih beh wù* ee beh woo	800	八百	*bah* „ ba „
160	一百六	*ih beh lúh* ee beh loo	900	九百	*giu* „ geeoo „
170	一百七	*ih beh tsih* ee beh chee	1,000	一千	*ih tsien* ee chee'en
180	一百八	*ih beh bah* ee beh ba	10,000	一萬	*ih wán* ee wan
190	一百九	*ih beh giu* ee beh geeoo	100,000	十萬	*shĭh wán* shirr wan
200	二百	*er beh* ur beh	1,000,000	一兆	*ih djào* ee jow

ORDINAL

1st	第一	*di ih* dee ee	6th	第六	*di lúh* dee loo
2nd	第二	*di er* dee ur	7th	第七	*di tsih* dee chee
3rd	„ 三	*di san* dee san	8th	„ 八	*di báh* dee ba
4th	„ 四	*di szi* dee siz	9th	„ 九	*di giu* dee geeoo
5th	„ 五	*di wú* dee woo	10th	„ 十	*di shĭh* dee shirr

MONEY.

The unit of currency for Chinese and foreign commerce is the *Tael*, which is not a coin but a *weight*, viz. a Chinese *ounce* (=1⅓ oz. Av.) of *silver*. Taels varying in weight, value, etc., are, however, used in different parts of the Empire, those in most general use being as follow:

1. The *Haikwan* or *Customs tael*, an arbitrary standard of currency in which all Maritime Customs duties are paid, but not employed for other commercial transactions.

2. The *Kuping* or *Treasury tael*, nominally uniform throughout the Empire, in which all Government taxes and duties apart from the Customs are reckoned, also those paid in copper *cash* or in kind.

3. The *Tsaoping* or *Shanghai tael*, in which foreign exchange rates are quoted by the banks in Shanghai.

These *taels* and others are interchangeable, but only by a complicated method of calculation; approximately

100 *Haikwan taels* =111·40 *Shanghai taels*, or 101·642 *Kuping taels*;
and 100 *Kuping taels* = 109·60 *Shanghai taels*.

BANK-NOTES.

Notes are issued by the branches of foreign banks, and by many native and provincial banks, in various multiples of the tael and dollar in the local currencies, of from 5 to 100 dollars, etc.

SILVER COINS.

Silver *dollars* are commonly employed for domestic and retail transactions, varying in different parts of the Empire and fluctuating in value; e.g. there are the Mexican dollar (Shanghai and neighbourhood), the Hongkong and Straits dollar (British), and the old Spanish or Carolus dollar, besides numerous Chinese dollars. These are interchangeable, but at fluctuating rates of exchange. The relative values of local dollars and local taels also fluctuate. There are besides 5, 10 and 20 cent pieces in circulation, nominally $\frac{1}{20}$, $\frac{1}{10}$ and $\frac{1}{5}$ dollar respectively. The approximate values are:

	English.	American.
Mexican dollar	2s.	50 cents
20-cent piece	5d.	10 ,,
10-cent ,, ...	2½d.	5 ,,
5-cent ,, ...	1¼d.	2 ,,

In addition there are great numbers of copper coins—the popular currency—of two kinds, viz. *10-cash* pieces or cents, and *1-cash* pieces; the latter made with a square hole through the middle by means of which they are strung in rolls of a hundred, ten rolls to a string, for tender. The value is very low and fluctuates, the *Shanghai tael* being now (1914) equal to 1700-1800 *cash*.

English & American Money with Chinese Equivalents.

English.	American.	Chinese.
£10 0 0	= $50·00	= $100·00
8 0 0 ...	40·00 ...	80·00
3 0 0 ...	15·00 ...	30·00
1 0 0 ...	5·00 ...	10·00
16 0 ...	4·00 ...	8.00
£0 2 6	= $0·62	= $1·25
1 0 ...	25 ...	51
6 ...	12 ...	25
1 ...	2 ...	4
0½ ...	1 ...	2

WEIGHTS & MEASURES.

WEIGHTS.

English.	Chinese.	Chinese.	English.
1 oz. av.	= ·75 *tael* (or 7.5 *chin*)	1 *fên* (or *candareen*)	= 5·833 gr.
1 lb. (16 oz.)	= ·75 *chin* (or 12 *taels*)	1 *ch'ien* (*mace* = 10 *fên*)	= 58·33 gr.
1 qr. (28 lb.)	= ·21 *tan* or *picul* (or 21 *chin*)	1 *liang* (*tael* = 10 *ch'ien*	= 583·3 gr. (1⅓ oz. av.*)
1 cwt. (112 lb.)	= ·84 *tan* (or 84 *chin*)	1 *chin* (*kin* or *catty* = 16 *liang*)	= 1⅓ lb. av.*
1 ton (20 cwt.)	= 16·8 *tan*	1 *tan* (*picul* = 100 *chin*)	= 133⅓ lb.*

* Fixed by Treaty for purposes of Foreign trade; in native trade the *chin* varies from 12 to 42 5 oz., and the number of *chins* to the *tan* from 90 to 280.

LENGTH.

English.	Chinese.	Chinese.	English.
1 inch ...	= 7·092 *fên*	1 *fên* ...	= ·141 inch
1 foot (12 in.)	= 8·51 *ts'un*	1 *ts'un* (10 *fên*)	= 1·41 ,,
1 yard (3 ft.)	= 2·553 *ch'ih*	1 *ch'ih** (10 *ts'un*)	= 14·1 in. (fixed for foreign trade)
1 furlong (220 yards) ...	= 56·166 *chang*	1 *chang* (10 *ch'ih*)	= 11 ft. 9 in.
1 mile (8 fur.)	= 2·496 *li*	1 *li* (180 *chang*)	= 705 yds. (3 fur. 8 po. 1 yd.)

* The *ch'ih* (Chinese *foot*) varies in practice from 8·6 to 27·8 inches.

CAPACITY.

Commodities, even fluids, e.g. oil, spirits, etc., are commonly sold by weight; measures of capacity are sometimes used for rice and other grain.

The *Tow*, holding from 6⅓ to 10 *chin* (*catty*) of rice, has an official capacity, for purposes of tribute, of 10·31 litres (about 2·315 gallons), but its capacity varies very greatly in different parts of the Empire.

POSTAL RATES FROM CHINA.

British Post office. *To United Kingdom:—*

LETTERS.—4 c. for each ounce or 20 grammes.

POST CARDS.—4 c., reply double.

BOOKS, NEWSPAPERS, &c.—2 c. per oz. (Single papers to British Possessions and some foreign countries, 2 c. per 4 oz.)

PARCELS.—Up to 3 lb., 60 c.; 3-7 lb., $1·20; 7-11 lb., $1·80.

To Countries in the Postal Union:—

LETTERS.—First ounce, 10 c. Each additional ounce, 6 c.

POST CARDS and NEWSPAPERS as above.

Chinese Post-office. *To U.K.:—*

LETTERS.—4 c. per 20 grammes.

POST CARDS.—1 c. single, 2 c. double.

NEWSPAPERS.—2 c. per 50 grammes.

To Postal Union Countries:—

LETTERS.—First 20 grammes, 10 c.; each additional 20 grammes, 6 c.

POST CARDS.—4 c. single, 8 c. double.

NEWSPAPERS.—2 c. per 50 grammes.

INDEX.